I0100669

THE BEQUEST

Nicolette Linden

The Enhanced Edition

To

my Severest Critic.

This work would not be what it is, without you.

Thank you.

The Bequest

This is a work of fiction.

Any resemblance to events, locales, names or persons, living or dead, is purely accidental or is used fictionally.

Oh God, Horatio ... tell my story.
Shakespeare, *Hamlet*, Act V, Scene ii

Strumming my pain with his fingers...
Singing my life with his words...
Telling my whole life with his words...
Roberta Flack, *Killing Me Softly*, 1973

The purpose of art is to remold nature and life so that it offers such complete harmony in itself that it does not point beyond its own limits but is an ultimate unity through the harmony of its parts.
Hugo Muensterberg, *The Photoplay: A Psychological Study*, 1916

I am he as you are he as you are me and we are all together.
The Beatles, *I am the Walrus*, 1967

Thus, it is ...overwhelmingly probable that we will always learn more about human life and human personality from novels than from scientific psychology.
Noam Chomsky, *Language and Problems of Knowledge: The Managua Lectures*, 1988

What is important is ...how the pieces in a film succeed one another, how they are structured.
Lev Kuleshov, Kuleshov on film: Writings of Lev Kuleshov. Trans. and Ed. Ronald Levaco, 1974

When a great tree falls...
When great souls die...
our eyes, briefly,
see with
a hurtful clarity.
Our memory,
suddenly sharpened,
examines, ...
Maya Angelou, *When a Great Tree Falls*, in *I Shall Not Be Moved*, 1990

Contents

Part 1 *The Preface*

    Prolog to the Preface   4

    The Preface   5

Part 2 *The Walrus* (A Five-Act Play)

    Act 1 (The Spark)   22

    Act 2 (The Expansion)   60

    Act 3 (The Regression)   133

    Act 4 (The Second Expansion)   181

    Act 5 (The Engagement)   211

    Notes   215

Part 3 *The Confession*

    Introduction, [3a]   216

    My Confession (A Two-Person Play), [3b]   222

    Reprise, [3c]   259

Part 4 Epilog   264

    [Jillian's] *Journal*,   265

    Items 1-6   265

    Item 7 *My Other Confession*   271

Part 5 *Professor Seiden's Last Seminar* (*PSLS*)

    Nicolette's Preamble   280

    Lecture 1 Introduction and Definitions   281

    Lecture 2 Overview of *The Bequest*   301

Lecture 3 (A double lecture) Overview continued, and micro-structural examination of *The Preface* — 322

Lecture 4 *The Walrus*, Act 1 — 346

Lecture 5 *The Walrus*, Act 2 — 354

Lecture 6 *The Walrus*, Acts 3-5 — 370

Lecture 7 Jillian's *The Confession* — 381

Part 1

Prolog to The Preface

The package came with a brief note. I read the documents. I cried. For so many reasons. I read them again and again, and I cried and laughed each time. Then I laughed and cried, for so many reasons.

I gave a month's notice to my employer. I told them that if they wished to keep me on —I was a chemical engineer— I would go to half-time. No negotiating. They accepted.

I had decided that I could live off that much income, plus my modest savings, plus child support. I would become a writer. I had to.

Morton was so smart not to give me my bequest in person. He knew that I would need to process it alone, with no distraction, not even conversation with him. But I am getting ahead of myself. Way ahead.

The Preface

When I was an embryo, my mother did not know she was pregnant, and my father ...well, he's another story. Actually, no, he's very much a part of this story. Mom —Jillian— was very smart emotionally and interpersonally. Her personality could be ninety percent described by a small set of adjectives: "kind, willing to put others ahead of herself, and modest." Professionally, she was a social worker–therapist.

By the way, call me Nicolette.

To give you an idea of Mom's emotional IQ, when I went off to college she placed near the bottom of my stuff, in a makeshift plain white paper wrapping on which she had neatly printed the words, "If ... insist," as if it were a miniature-novel, a three-pack of condoms. Aside from her cleverness, this "title" was relevant to the beginning of "the novel" of my sexuality. Not immediately, but eventually, of course. By the way, you should know that I did not have any experience of that kind at that time. She was so unobtrusive, so clever, so subtle. Like a blessing, but only under the right conditions.

My father was a much more complex individual whose personality requires several sets of descriptors. I get this mostly via Mom, of course, but it will be borne out. You'll see. I'll give you two examples right now so as not to tease you: my cousin told me that his friend had once asked him to clarify this favorite uncle who he occasionally spoke of, so highly but so paradoxically. My cousin told him, "I'd have to talk for at least three minutes." I also asked father's friend, David, to tell me about my father. "How much time do you have?" he jokingly asked. In short, it isn't just my impression based on Mom's conveyance. It was him.

Mom —Jillian— told me that my father was extremely important to her: "Much more than just a lover," was the way she put it. "He impregnated my mind." That is *some* statement! It is not an over-estimate however, as you will see when you read her work, *The Confession*.

Morton, who you will meet later —who father dubbed a literary "demi-god"— tried to help Mom get her work published. But despite his prestigious reputation the manuscript was rejected. "It is impossible to categorize. Is it a story surrounding a play or plays? Is it narrative or drama? Which form prevails?" Agents admitted, grudgingly or guiltily, that they just didn't know where to place it, or who was the audience. "It is beautiful, but it's so precariously balanced." Morton would rejoin, "Of course! That's the beauty of it! Part of the beauty! Both pieces emanate from the WuShi centerpoint, separately and together! What don't you get about that?" And he added, "How often do you come across works like this?!" Yet, triple nyet; no, no, Nyet! No publisher would take a chance on it. "Well done, ...but No."

Mom knew this would be the case, and she was okay with it. In the marvelous dialog between her and Morton that you will read momentarily, she sounds accepting of the fact that it cannot be categorized, and is therefore, perhaps, unpublishable. She thought her market might be as an audiobook instead. (Her fantasy was for Tracey Ullman to voice her part, Robin Williams, William's, and for Jeremy Irons to play Morton.) She posted the document —her *Confession*— to Morton, as promised, later that afternoon ... the day of her *Confession* visit with him ...the day she completed it, and her life.

Her *Confession* is a symphony of homages: to William, to Morton, and to several important others. More important than that though, her play was a challenge to herself. I think it accurate to say that her late-found ability to create that document —her story-play-story— is my father's spiritual "bequest" to her, as much as I am his physical "bequest" to her. I name this document, *The Bequest*, because so many "bequests" have been involved in its provenance. Morton re-bequeathed it to me, as Jillian had entrusted him to do, when I reached age thirty. Yin into Yang into Yin, revolving. This work, *as-a-whole,* is mine. I have had to synthesize her work, his work, and Morton's commentary on both of their works, into an organic whole. *Ecce opus.*

She, Mom, would not let me read it, *The Walrus*, until I turned thirty! She knew that I needed ...well, you'll see, it will become obvious. I could not possibly have understood it the way it should be understood, and I might have been freaked out. Would have been. We often resent parents for under-appreciating our capacities, and sometimes I did, and we are often right; but sometimes we are wrong. And I was wrong. Had Mom caved, I would have been harmed. As she said, —attributing this to Father— "in a child's development, No, is as important as Yes." In view of the complex relationships that swirl through *The Walrus* and especially the characters' intense level of honesty —to say nothing of the unflinching imagery per se— she was right.

But I didn't make it easy for her!

We had had some discussions when she was working on parts of *The Confession* but since it referred back to *The Walrus,* she would not let me read it! Why not? "The dramatic tension between the characters could not be understood without knowledge of *The Walrus,*" she offered. "*The Walrus* is the *eminence gris* behind my work." But she would not let me read *that* until I attained age 30. I would have to wait. What a paltry explanation! It was *no* explanation. I didn't understand. And, what an *idiotic* name!

She wanted it that way. "It needs to be that way," she said, adding, "I'm mad, 'only north by northwest." She named the pivotal material obscurely because she wished to prevent the reader from any connotations prior to entering its vortex. "The idiotic title becomes completely understandable," she said, "if one loops back to the citation quotes."

She had let me read that one page. "No one pays attention to those," I told her. "And there are too many of them anyway! Who has six citations? Ridiculous!" "Some will," she replied, "They'll return to check them out because of a sub-surface echo."

"You're trusting your reader too much," I argued, "and why do you insist on this convoluted route?" She returned obliquely, "I have my reasons," and offered, again obliquely, that, "Hamlet didn't explain. He dropped hints like, 'mad north-northwest,'" adding this as if she were giving me a comprehensible clarification. She further added, "When you read it a few times, you'll see. You'll get it. ...Or you won't."

Some clarification!

This was okay with her, and I've increasingly grown to respect her attitude. This still surprises me emotionally, although I fully understand it intellectually. I've learned that her choice was more than mere artistic license. It —the idiotic title— originally had two different provisional titles. "They gave away too much," Mom explained much, much later. And she was right. I now understand. So: *The Walrus*.

She said —more like admitted— that she wanted a loving reader to feel and, hopefully, to recognize every stitch of her artistic needlework. But if not, they should at least enjoy a rollercoaster ride of a read.

Here is an outtake, undated, that I found in her drawer along with *The Walrus* and *The Confession*, all of which I later transferred to a safe deposit box.

Morton & Jillian Discuss the Title

MORTON: Remember our discussion about your Work, your untitled Work?
JILLIAN: I certainly do.
M: What did you think about it?
J: I gave it a lot of thought. But I just couldn't do it. I couldn't come up with one.
M: Well, *The History of Love* is taken. (Both smile)
J: (Long pause) Morton ...what is your definition of love?

M: Now there's a pivot! What a change of direction!

J: Answer me, please. It's relevant. Try to.

M: I can't give you a good definition any more than anybody else can. I suppose it's like the Supreme Court's definition of pornography: "I can't define it, but I know it when I see it."

J: Would you believe a good definition has been offered?

M: No, I would not.

J: In five words.

M: I would certainly not!

J: Well ...how's this: *The Willing Interpenetration of Souls*?

Morton: (Slowly) The willing interpenetration of souls. da-Dah-da, Dah-da-Dah-da-Dah-da, da-Dah. ...Acceptable. (Pensive) And conceptually.

J: (Nods)

M: When did you compose that?

J: William.

M: Oh. ...I see.

J: When he thought about puzzling things, he thought them deeply; he likened it to solving an equation. Often, he couldn't do it, you know, with big questions, but sometimes he came up with real gems. "I like to put 'em in a nutshell, if possible," he told me. (M thinking, J sensing mood)

J: So, you see, only *WloS* will fit.

M: Why? ...No! Would you rather it be an homage to William, or to get the play published and produced?

J: In my heart, an homage.

M: (Quizzical, disapproving glance)

J: I see your disapproval.

M: Mmmm. Look, Jillie ....the concision is good, surprisingly good, really. But you still have the practical matter of getting your work published.

J: I'd love for it to be published or produced, if it can be, but I care more about maintaining its integrity.

M: An almost–as–good title is not a sell-out. The Work itself will demonstrate the definition of love, the "Willing Interpenetration." The *demonstration* is crucial, not the title.

J: (Pensive) Hmmm.

M: Look, Jillie, *Interpenetration of Souls* is simply too much. It has a mellow philosophical ring, but it's too tendentious for a title. And —just in case you're thinking about it—*The Growth of Love* can't work either. For many and obvious reasons.

J: (Smiles) I will only change the title if I can find something equal to it, or better, if that's possible. (Long silence)

J: Return to a word you used just before. ...I know what you meant from context, but I'm not really sure what that word means, "tendentious."

M: (Mischievous smile, head bobbing and jive finger gesturing). In *this* moment it means, heavy, man, too heavy! Too intellectual. Too much for the reader to bear. No intrigue.

J: (Laughs) Morton, you are the youngest old man I know!

M: (Smiles) You run with the wrong old men.

J: Okay, Okay, you can stop your teasing here.

M: (Enjoying the tease, continues) And how many of them do you *run* with?

J: (Deciding not to fight his tease) Not many. And none like *you* ...don't worry! (Pause) Morton. I'll think about it again. Stop teasing me. I'll rethink it.

I love that conversation. The level of respect and honesty, the give and take, the not backing down. I guess Mom figured it didn't belong in her *Confession*, that it would have disrupted the main train of thought; and if so, she was right.

Mom and I had a great relationship. So, I was more than annoyed by her refusal. I was pissed! I don't like that expression, but everyone uses it today, so I'll use it; but I don't like it. I was offended. I wheedled and cajoled and outright begged her to share both documents with me. I rationalized that it would give me insight into my father and his influence on her and their relationship. She refused. Categorically!

It was the only time in my life I was angry with her in a way that stayed with me for a few months. But now I know she was right. I would do the same for my daughters. I would not let them read *The Walrus* until they are thirty or maybe —on a stretch—

twenty-five. Mom had pointed out that I am like him, Father —I always referred to him that way— in many ways. How, for example? He would have pressed himself to answer the question, Why thirty? And when I now ask myself, Why that number? I say, "Not until they had had at least two significant relationships, or had reached thirty years of age." For them to put all of it into perspective, even to believe parts of it they would need both experience and maturity. I didn't have them then. No one my age *could* have. It's just as simple as that, and Mom was right, and I was furious.

I didn't give up, though. I tried to appeal to her on intellectual grounds when all else failed:

NICOLETTE: Why can't I read it, *The Walrus*? Or what you're working on now.
JILLIAN: I've told you, when your thirty. And this wouldn't make sense without having read *The Walrus*.
N: Well why can't I read just the first part of what you're writing?
J: Because you can't. I don't want you to, yet. Because you need more maturity to process it. And it all relates to *The Walrus*

anyway. (Then adding, in an encouraging and idiotically upbeat voice) ...When I'm dead.

N: (Matching upbeat voice) Oh, great! Something to look forward to! ...Come on! You always say I'm so mature. Mature beyond my years.

J: You are.

N: So...?

J: You need more maturity. And, besides, it's so unusual you'd think it preposterous.

N: What you're writing now or, *The Walrus*?

J: *The Walrus*.

N: Oh, "preposterous." That's a reason? You want *preposterous*? How about *King Lear*? *King Lear* is preposterous! A man successfully runs a kingdom, then goes daft in old age and demands that his daughters vie to show him which of them loves him most? Now *there's* a preposterous beginning for you! Utter nonsense. Almost deranged. And that play worked out well despite it, don't you think?

J: It's not like that.

N: How about *Macbeth* ...witches! —really? And that worked out magnificently, don't you agree?

J: No, no, it's not like that!

N: So, what is it 'like'?

J: I won't tell you now. You wouldn't believe it if I did tell you. And it's too intensely personal. But it happened. The essence happened, in fact. And even if it were partly fiction, fiction can teach truth. Look what Mark Twain did in Huck Finn!

N: Mom, you're all over the map! You're on too many levels at once! Don't you want me to know you that intensely personally, Mom?

J: Yes. No. Not yet. Yes, I really do. But I won't give it to you now.

I'll spare you the next ten minutes of wheedling! Finally, Mom said, "I'm not discussing this further. You will understand, eventually."

So the argument went around and around and got nowhere. "When you're thirty." I was mystified and resentful for months.

But now I see and agree with her although I have to tell you that my best friend —who is much like Roberta, who you will meet just ahead in Act 2, Scene 2— proposed a disturbing counterargument. She felt that *The Walrus* should be *required* reading! In senior year of high school! Along with *Huck Finn* and *The Things They Carried*. I see her point. I half-agree with her.

Less than half.

Mom —Jillian— took decades to write it, her *Confession*, or to be able to write it. It germinated for that long, like one of those seeds that can withstand fire and drought, but then, under the right conditions, suddenly sprouts back to life. She never forgot her first spark, to share something with Morton and give him something he would relish. To make him proud of her. Life got in the way; like raising me and going to graduate school in her chosen field, which turned out not to be writing.

And perhaps she simply wasn't ready. Her writing is so complex. You'll see. Her play especially, requires constant focusing, defocusing, and refocusing. It requires a lot of work, but it flows and is a joy.

I read *The Walrus* five times the first day. I could hardly sleep that night! I read it at least twenty times the first month. Since then I've re-read it perhaps a hundred times. More, maybe. I know sections of it by heart. But I assure you that what Mom told each of her six widely-read reader–friends beforehand, is true: "There is no way anyone can get them, *The Walrus* and *The Confession,* on one read." What a sculptor must feel when warming, kneading, and folding clay, and then molding it into a form, and then remodeling that into another form, is what reading them feels like to me; and I *knew* the characters. *I* had to re-read it several times to get the overall perspective, the right coordinates, and then to figure out how she did what she did, Jillian, in the *My Confession* dialog.

Morton, "the demi-god," did not detect something in *The Walrus.* Yes, he had been misled by Jillian, but ...he might have wondered about something. I realize I am speaking vaguely now, and I don't usually permit myself to do that —forgive me— but I can't spoil *The Walrus* for you. And the *My Confession* part of *The Confession* is such a rotating mobile that it can give a reader vertigo. Even the demi-god's head was spinning in the verbal vortex that Jillian used and *had* to use in order to both progressively reveal and yet still conceal something from him. At the end of *My Confession*, *he* was hanging on to Mom's coattails, and Morton usually grasped everything the first time.

It is very different.

Oh yes, a P.S., sorry. Morton became so energized by Jillian's *Confession* that, for more than a year, he enthusiastically promoted Mom's work to various publishers. He even "went dysregulated" on his publisher, the one that had produced his book on Yeats. That book's critical acclaim and Morton's august reputation were to no avail.

They, *The Walrus* and *The Confession*, lay in a drawer for years, next to each other at the bottom of Jillian's pajama drawer. I transferred them to a safe deposit box when my kids —the twins, William and Roberta— got older. They, the two plays, had to be contained, metabolized, and subsumed into something else, integrated into something bigger. I have tried to do that with this, *this* this, *The Bequest.* Mom legally willed me the rights to both upon my reaching age thirty. Morton re-bequeathed it to me. I am doubly bequeathed, and doubly blessed. But it has gestated too long and I must deliver it. I must "bring it into the light."

A complex, soul-wrenching quilt, woven primarily from the two plays and secondarily from Morton's last Creative Writing Seminar, this, *The Bequest*, is my creation. It —this story— and they —the works mentioned above— shall lay in a safe deposit box no longer!

And ..."We have lift off."

Part 2

The Walrus

Cast of Characters

Jillian

William

Roberta

Caitlin, Roberta's sister

Haley and Marcella, friends of both sisters

Two other women, Jillian's friends

David and Charles, William's friends

Michael, William's brother

A Figure

ACT I

SCENE 1

(The Spark)

SETTING: The previous Friday night, Jillian and her two friends, and William and his friend David, were at a lower East Side bar with an open mic venue for comedians and musicians. All having a drink. William chatted her up, and she was pleased to chat back. He asked for her phone number and she gave it. This Saturday, they are at Jillian's place dipping and coloring Easter eggs for her nephew and niece. Conversation goes smoothly, back and forth for two hours, about family, more on Jillian's side, some personal history, some funny stories. Brunch.

JILLIAN What attracted you to me?

WILLIAM (Gathering) Now there's a question!
(Takes a few breaths) Your smile. Most of all, your smile. I love your smile. ...And your legs.

JILLIAN What about my smile? ...And I was wearing a long skirt that night!

WILLIAM You have the most open smile. When you laughed with your friends, it was so unaffected and unguarded. It charmed me. You were so open. ...Not like some girls, to make the point, "see how much fun I am?" followed by hair flip. Marketing, and usually phony.

JILLIAN And the other? You couldn't see much.

WILLIAM I could see your lower legs and a little more when you sat on the stool and crossed your legs. They are beautiful.

JILLIAN That runs in my family.

WILLIAM ...Then you must have me meet your family, soon. I mean the women. I couldn't care less if the men have nice legs or not.

JILLIAN (Laughs and playfully smacks his upper arm.) You're a dog. Say "woof."

(Long pause, silence comfortable)

JILLIAN You seem entirely comfortable coloring Easter eggs.

WILLIAM Sure. Why wouldn't I be?

JILLIAN I mean, this doesn't seem silly to you?

WILLIAM No. Why? I'm with you. We're having conversation, and we're going to delight your niece and nephew. What's silly?

Besides, later, following this, we're going to have raucous sex. (Big smile)

JILLIAN (Big smile) Oh are you ahead of yourself!

WILLIAM Playing....

JILLIAN Oh, okay....

WILLIAM (Smiles)

JILLIAN (Smiles back) I guess what I'm fishing for is for you to tell me something about your background. You've hardly mentioned anything about your background.

WILLIAM I didn't have a pleasant childhood, Jill, for the most part. So I don't talk about it much. And not until I really know the person who may be interested. Who wants to hear bad news?

JILLIAN (Pause) Do you believe in god?

WILLIAM (Totally surprised. Gathers.) Uhm, ...Yes.

(Waxing more enthusiastic) Yes.

(Emphatically) Yes! ...And in the Easter Bunny!

(Makes big eyes, appears sincere) ...And, in Santa Claus!

JILLIAN (Laughs, but uncertain)

WILLIAM (Holds her glance and says with rising enthusiasm) With all my heart and all my soul and all my might, I believe in Santa. He's my *fave*.

JILLIAN (Laughs) Oh, ...I see.

WILLIAM What sparked your question?

JILLIAN You seem so comfortable doing this, yet you've never indicated a religious or philosophical identity.

WILLIAM "Religious" or "philosophical?" I *love* when you use big words. It turns me on. It's like when you talk dirty when we make love.

JILLIAN We haven't made love!

WILLIAM No, but when we do, if we do, I want you to talk dirty, and to moan, and to tell me your most drastic desires and farthest-out fantasies. (Quick voice change to indifference) Or, equally, you can use big words and talk philosophy. (Smiles) Either one. Sex talk or philosophy, your choice.

JILLIAN Whoa, don't jump the gun!

WILLIAM (Smiles and pauses) I'm just playing, Jillie.

JILLIAN I thought so. I know. You're not defensive about this. Some people would be. Most people would just name a religion, you know, of background, even if they don't really believe in it. You know, mention it and forget it.

WILLIAM ...I have a rule of thumb. Get the hard stuff over with first. If the relationship survives, business or romantic, the rest will be easy, or at least easier. So, is my philosophy a deal-breaker?

JILLIAN No, not at all.

WILLIAM By religion? ...I'm secular. A Humanist.

JILLIAN What? That's a religion?

WILLIAM No, not exactly. You might say it's an orientation, like Daoism or Buddhism.

JILLIAN I don't know anything about them. What do you mean?

WILLIAM You don't really want to go into this. Do you?

JILLIAN Sure, why not?

WILLIAM You want to go right down to the marrow?

JILLIAN Yes. ...I think so. Like dogs. (Laughs, both smile)

WILLIAM . ...But remember, you asked for it.

JILLIAN I said, Yes. I mean it. I'm an adult.

WILLIAM Okay, Adult, but remember....

JILLIAN Um hmm. *Proceed*....

WILLIAM So, ...let's say you're at a prestigious award ceremony, or a game show contest, and a winner must be announced. There are three candidates for the *all–time* greatest *human* factor —not natural things like fire, flood or plague— that accounts for the most confusion, shame, guilt, self-delusion, fear of non-conforming neighbors, hatred of neighbors, killing of neighbors, direct pain and collateral suffering that people have inflicted on each other. ...What would you say that factor is?

JILLIAN I don't know. I've never asked myself anything like that!

WILLIAM (Purposely ignoring and letting her see it) To help ...the semi-finalist contestants are: Ordinary human greed, Nationalism, and Religion. ...Which would you choose?

JILLIAN (Gestures, I don't know)

WILLIAM And, (Ignoring and answering the original question) ...the winner is....

(Mimes breaking the seal of an envelope. Then, in an ecstatically happy voice.)

...We have a *winner*! The *all–time* most divisive factor! Religion! Congratulations, Religion!

JILLIAN (Pause, uncertain, gathering) I thought they all preached love at bottom.

WILLIAM You should study them more deeply. Your study would surprise you.

JILLIAN (Perplexed) Oh.

WILLIAM Jillie, listen, I celebrate Christmas. Even though I'm an atheist or a nontheist, better word, I celebrate it because I love the fact that people stop thinking only about themselves long enough to think about other people, however briefly.

JILLIAN So, that's good.

WILLIAM I just said so. But that —thinking what to do for others or what to buy them to make them happy— is a tradition and has nothing to do with group identity or theology. You don't need religion to do that. A society can encourage people to do that without a lot of mystifying stuff–and–nonsense. You can be a good person without drinking the Kool-Aid.

...And, oh yes, I love the colors and some of the music. And the smell of pine trees.

JILLIAN Okay, so you're comfortable painting Easter eggs with me.

WILLIAM Of course. I've already told you so. I'm with you, finding out about you. Looking at you, hearing your voice, and ...hoping to see your legs again.

JILLIAN (Fakes anger) Stop that! Can't you stay serious for a while without bringing up my legs?

WILLIAM (Pretended stupidity) Duhhh. No.

...Sure, okay, but only briefly.

(Both laugh)

And —I'm back to serious now, so credit me— we're doing something that will delight some children, your relatives. I love that.

JILLIAN Good.

WILLIAM I'm a good person, and "God" has nothing to do with that.

JILLIAN I was always taught that they ran together.

WILLIAM Well ...do they? I'm a good person, and a nontheist. And, just by the by, I'm not militant.

JILLIAN I've always been leery of that word ...people who were "atheists."

WILLIAM Why?! Some people have been taught to be afraid of the mere word, "atheist." They've been taught —mindwashed, actually— that abandoning their Nonsense–of–Origin is being "disloyal," even traitorous, that it's dissing their parents and their background. But there's no basis for that.

And It's also an implicit threat, really. Does a fish see water? Whether consciously promoted or taken for granted, it's a form of in-house and in-community bullying. Skipping a lot of steps ...one can respect one's background and parents yet be pleased and proud to have evolved beyond it and them.

JILLIAN I've never heard a perspective like yours before. I'll be thinking about this for a while.

WILLIAM Good.

JILLIAN What did you mean by, "not a militant?"

WILLIAM Simplified ...I get something out of my understandings, and I don't try to impose my worldview on anyone. If others get something out of their beliefs and rituals, I'm okay with that. "Not a militant?" I don't try to persuade others to shed their beliefs, but I sure don't want them imposing theirs on me. ..."Live and let live."

JILLIAN Okay. ...My question bit off more than I anticipated.

WILLIAM Yup. It's a heady bone we're gnawing on. Too heady. Let's drop this for now.

JILLIAN Agreed.

WILLIAM Show me your legs. ...Draw your skirt up.

JILLIAN *Will* you stop that! (Laughs, both laugh)

WILLIAM A little, ...*please*. Draw your skirt up,

JILLIAN Stop that!

WILLIAM (Looks at her but holds her eyes) Okay.

JILLIAN (Wanting to co-pilot the conversation) But how *would* you define yourself, if someone asked you?

WILLIAM I've already told you, but if *someone* asked —*you* maybe?— (smiles) I'd say, (purposely complicating the matter) I'm a Spinozistic Buddhist. ...Is that better?

JILLIAN A what?!

WILLIAM (Pretended simplification) A Spinozan Buddhist.

JILLIAN What? What's that? What are you talking about?

WILLIAM Why do people have to pin others with these tribal labels, Jillie? They only serve to divide. And then, whoever conquers, that tribe wins and becomes Chief Bully for a while.

JILLIAN A Buddhist? What kind of Buddhist?

WILLIAM I was joking.

JILLIAN Oh.

WILLIAM (Encouraging) But if forced, of all available choices, I would say I'm Buddhist in spirit.

JILLIAN Tell me more about yourself. Something deep.

WILLIAM (Chuckles) *This* is pretty deep, don't you think?

JILLIAN I know. (Laughs at self) It is, but I like hearing you talk.

WILLIAM Oh, ...keep me talking. (Chuckles) Okay.

JILLIAN Yes. I really like listening to you. The way you talk ... speak.

WILLIAM Okay, I'll tie two strands together; entertain you and tell you a moment from my history. I was forced to declare one once, a religion. I mentioned earlier that I have an Indian friend, Sunil, from college.

JILLIAN Yes.

WILLIAM Before I went to India to visit him, I had to fill out the Indian visa application. It requires a statement of profession of religion.

JILLIAN They do?

WILLIAM Yup. You wouldn't believe it, but they do. Who would think they could get away with that? So, I filled out the form and sent it in with "none" written on it. They sent it back, with yellow highlight through the words, "religious profession." I called their document agency, CKGS, on West Twenty-third Street. They told me it must be filled out entirely as they specified. No discussion. "Different culture, different regs." So, forced choice, I filled out the new form: Buddhist.

JILLIAN Really? I like that.

WILLIAM I do too. If I died there, they could put my remains along with a simple note and float it down a river with a candle, like the Japanese do. I like that.

JILLIAN I like when you share things like that with me. Thanks.

WILLIAM You're welcome. I must be going very shortly.

JILLIAN So soon?

WILLIAM Yes. I have to meet David to play racquetball. We have a court at 3 o'clock.

JILLIAN Right. Okay.

(They go to door, first kiss, pull away, look at each other, hug and kiss again on cheeks; he returns, then holds her face in his hands and kisses her cheeks again, and then, after a pause, mouth, lightly.)

WILLIAM (About to exit) Oh, when I see you next time would you like me to bring over some songs on a playlist I've compiled?

JILLIAN Sure! What kind of songs?

WILLIAM Vintage '50s and early '60s. I've curated them. I give a tiny intro to each. The greatest slow dance music ever made. The most romantic.

JILLIAN That sounds great. Give me a sneak preview.

WILLIAM That'll spoil it.

JILLIAN No it won't! We'll dance to them, and that'll be great.

WILLIAM Okay, a peek. So, I've arranged it chronologically from, *"The Closer You Are,"* earliest '50s, through *"One Summer Night"* and *"You Cheated, You Lied "* —my all-time favorite— to early '60s Motown, Diana Ross and the Supremes, *"Will You Still Love Me Tomorrow"* and *"Baby Love, My Baby Love."* I have them on a disc, do you have a disc player that works?

JILLIAN Yes. That sounds great. I can't wait to hear it! I love to dance, and my disc player has a good sound system. So, next Saturday evening ...about seven? I'll make dinner. What would you like?

WILLIAM I don't know ...You know what Bob Hope replied when they asked him where he'd like to be buried?

JILLIAN No. (Gathering) Of *course* not! How *could* I?

WILLIAM ..."Surprise me."

JILLIAN (Laughs and gives a smile; they hug goodbye again, cheek kisses again.)

ACT I
SCENE 2

Aroma of Thai food wafting into the hallway.

WILLIAM Hi. That smells so good! (Double cheek kisses. Hands her an oversized floral bouquet.) For you.

JILLIAN Oh, this is so nice of you. Come in, I'll put them in water. I love tulips, they herald spring and look so sweet. Where did you get them in *all* these colors? And what an *arrangement*!

WILLIAM In the Flower District. A former patient manages a shop there. He told me not to hesitate if I ever wanted something special.

JILLIAN That's so nice of him. This is spectacular!

(Small talk: nephew and niece, Easter eggs, racquetball match, David; over dinner and beer, a bit of talk about current job stuff. After dinner, they go into the living room.)

WILLIAM So, here it is, my playlist.

JILLIAN I'll put on two candles. One has a scent. Do you like Patchouli?

WILLIAM. Not really. I prefer sandalwood, if you have that. That's a better bet.

(While Jillian is putting the disc in and adjusting the sound, William comes over to her and embraces her from behind and kisses her neck. Then he turns her around and starts to dance with her, five dances in a row, slow, very slow, each luxuriating being in each other's arms; pause for a cold drink, then resume dancing.)

WILLIAM I love holding you.

JILLIAN Mmmm, and I, you.

WILLIAM I love feeling your body changes.

JILLIAN What do you mean?

WILLIAM A couple of times I felt, or think I felt, some sexual energy ripples.

JILLIAN (Pushes away a bit, big smile plus frown) Come *on* now! You're just *suggesting* something to me.

WILLIAM No, no I'm not. Did you not have a thought or desire?

JILLIAN When?

WILLIAM If I nail it ...you owe me.

JILLIAN *No* I don't! Owe you *what*? *Stop* that! Tell me. Let's just *see*.

WILLIAM Okay, but you owe me.... During *"You Cheated,"* at least once. When they were singing, "Oh, what can I do, but just, keep on loving you?"

JILLIAN Did you take a course in *mind reading*!

WILLIAM Body reading.

JILLIAN No! They don't teach *that*!

WILLIAM They don't. Yet. But I pick these things up. At least sometimes. Often.

JILLIAN (Just looks at him)

WILLIAM Is that a confession you're hiding, under your eyes and cheeks?

JILLIAN (Smiles but turns her eyes away) Yes.

WILLIAM I *like* this. This could turn into a *most* interesting conversation. But let's sit down now. I want to hold you and snuggle and kiss you.

(Jillian walks over to the sofa. Music continues, William embraces her, and she molds herself into him. They kiss. Hands exploring only faces and sides of bodies. William pulls away to assess. Jillian is pleased. They make out like that for minutes. He kisses her again and uses his weight to push her onto her back on the sofa. She yields. They continue to kiss more. Neck, face, ears. Jillian feels his weight on her, and she relaxes her legs. William is delighted. She is pleased, too. No other boyfriend had enjoyed getting to know her so gradually. Jillian likes the way he feels, grooving into her. William presses into her, does not go for more. Kissing, caressing arms and sides of body. No breasts. Because he is not going for more, Jillian relaxes and trusts more. They groove. She knows he is feeling her, and she lets herself feel him, each tactually imaging the other's special places.

William stops there, pulls her up with him, not wanting to come like that, there, then, and sits up. Recovery. Long silence.)

WILLIAM Let's have one more dance and then I'll leave.

JILLIAN That sounds good.

(Both dance to "*Will You Still Love Me Tomorrow*," knowing that the other is feeling the other's body fully, through their clothing.)

WILLIAM Good night.

(Kisses her face, all around, eyes, too, and ears)

JILLIAN Hmmm, you make me purr like a kitten. I'll sleep well tonight. Good night.

ACT I

SCENE 3

Having had a great date, many laughs, walking, talking, museum, shopping, dinner, Jillian and William are in her apartment, talking, saying goodnight.

(William embraces her; Jillian happily reciprocates. They kiss and make out. It goes unhurriedly. Leisurely. Jillian is glad for this. Relieved and a little surprised. No other boyfriend has been like this. They continue making out for a long time. Jillian enjoying William's sustained enjoyment of her, his attention and his very gradual approach to her body. William is reading every aspect of her reactions, breath, anticipation of his next move or not, and of her move or not. They keep kissing. William caresses her back and arms and lower back, and then ass, but does not go further. She senses his restraint and is briefly perplexed by it; happy, but confused. He pulls away and looks at her, to relax her, and also to assess. They kiss again, and William takes her in fully. Jillian senses this and responds. But at a certain moment she pulls away. They separate briefly, look at each other, William assessing. Cannot sustain the rising passion? Jillian slightly embarrassed, does not know what to say.)

WILLIAM What happened?

JILLIAN (Heart racing) I don't know. Maybe I got a little scared.

WILLIAM Of what? Why?

JILLIAN I don't know.

(Silence)

WILLIAM I want to know.

JILLIAN I think I got scared.

(Sensing a plunge in his mood, she reaches to reconnect to him)

I'd tell you if I knew.

WILLIAM This disturbs me. It makes me sad for you. And for me.

(They pull away, talk a bit more)

JILLIAN I don't know why. I'm sorry.

WILLIAM You know, it is probably best to stop here.

JILLIAN What do you mean? Stop seeing each other?

WILLIAM No, no. Just take a breather. To process.

JILLIAN Are you mad, upset?

WILLIAM No. I'll call you.

JILLIAN Will you?

WILLIAM Yes. And please don't do that Jillie. If I tell you I will do something, I will do it. ...If I didn't want to see you again, I would tell you. Nicely, but I would tell you. It's not that. I want to process what happened. What just happened.

JILLIAN (Restraining emotion, not understanding, saying with her eyes, "give me another kiss.")

WILLIAM (Smiles, gladly pulls her to him, and they kiss again, and he caresses her back, and ass — to reassure her that he does desire her. Then smiles again.) Goodnight.

ACT I

SCENE 4

A week later, more good conversation, dinner, a walk in a park, and back at Jillian's place.

(Snuggle and kiss on the sofa. William embraces her and again slowly works her up, caressing her back and arms and ass. Jillian is pleased. William starts to slip his hand under her arm to caress her breast, and she releases her arm to allow him. He caresses her, alternately gently and then firmly, and also stopping to look at her and then resume kissing. Jillian noticeably relaxes more. He shifts and caresses her other breast. Jillian thinks, I love the way he touches me. They continue making out. Jillian breaks the rhythm. They look at each other. William is uncertain of her mood, wanting more, but restraining. They break, talk a little, and then resume kissing. This time William pulls back a little to free his hand to unbutton a button on her blouse. She allows it. They kiss more, and William re-caresses her neck and back and ass. Then looks at her and kisses her more and slips his index finger into her bra. Jillian is pleased, and then is surprised at how much more pleasurable what he is doing is compared to other experiences. He circles her areola, and then kisses her more passionately, while simultaneously pushing her bra down to expose her breast and play with her nipple with his index finger and thumb. He gently pulls her nipple, too, and gently twists it. Jillian laughs and giggles.)

WILLIAM What?

JILLIAN I like what you were doing. No one's ever touched me that way and made me feel that good. You make me feel very good.

WILLIAM (Very happy to hear that) Good!

(They kiss more. Jillian wonders if he is going to go for more and how she will react if he does. William kisses her more but again feels something. Stops.)

JILLIAN What? Why are you pulling away?

WILLIAM You lost step with me. We weren't in sync.

JILLAN I think I was.

WILLIAM I don't. And I've learned to trust myself in these things. I can be wrong, but in this I'm not. You weren't.

JILLIAN I'm sorry.

WILLIAM For what?

JILLIAN For making you upset.

WILLIAM Jill, that's less important than you figuring out what you were really feeling. I want us to be completely in sync, the experience is so much richer that way.

JILLIAN (Perturbed, but forces herself to say something that will hold him for the resumption.) I had a flash about a previous boyfriend.

WILLIAM *That* I believe. And I'm glad you're starting to admit to me. I don't want to rush you into anything, but I also don't want to feel like I'm a dentist extracting teeth.

JILLIAN (Almost laughs, but sad) I felt something, but I can't say more. I don't know myself what it is.

WILLIAM Thanks for that, and that's even more reason that we should take a breather, to reflect. (Smiles, pulls her to him and kisses her face, a lot) Not to break off. I really like you. I want to know you completely. Need to. That's how I am with someone I really like. Let's call it a night and talk about this next time.

JILLIAN (Big, free smile. Relieved and happy that he mentions a next time. Hugs and kisses him.)

WILLIAM Good night.

ACT I

SCENE 5

Afternoon concert, one drink in a trendy downtown bar, then drive into the early evening until they reach a wooded, romantic spot.

(Jillian pleased at his sequencing of venues and his conveying not expecting a date to be "repaid" by sex. William is pleased to be giving to Jillian and enjoys seeing her relax more and more. They walk for a bit before sunset, but it is buggy where they are, and they return to the car. Debate, on William's part, "Go for more, or talk? In what order?" Decides, 'talk first.')

WILLIAM Have you figured out what happened?

JILLIAN What do you mean?

WILLIAM I need you to open yourself to me Jillian, fully. I want you fully or not at all. Your mind. When we were kissing, something happened at a certain point, and I didn't like what I felt. I felt you pull away emotionally. I asked you to think about that. Did you?

JILLIAN Some.

WILLIAM Yes....

JILLIAN I got scared.

WILLIAM Of what?

JILLIAN I'm not sure. I think because you were going to rush me into something I wasn't sure I wanted to do.

WILLIAM That sounds right. Your mood was conflicted. I picked that up.

JILLIAN I was anticipating what more you might want me to do, or do to me, and that I'd be both glad for it and not.

WILLIAM Good. We're getting somewhere. "Glad," I understand. "Not," I don't.

(Long pause, medley of blues playing softly in the background.)

Jillian, our whole deal is based on your being completely honest with me. Work to find the answer. I'll be that way with you too.

JILLIAN It's not that I didn't want you to. I really like you. And we're both adults, I know that, but....

WILLIAM You skipped to some other thought. Something conflicted you.

JILLIAN Yes.

WILLIAM What?

JILLIAN (Turns to him, imploring with her eyes to be understanding) Oh, William, do I have to say? I don't want to.

WILLIAM (Sensing mood) Yes, you do. But not right now. I feel where you're at. Eventually. When you're ready to.

JILLIAN Thank you.

(William hugs her and waits until her breath subsides, then kisses her cheek, and pulls her to him. She relaxes more. He kisses her. When he feels her return to herself, he kisses her again and puts his hand on her thigh near her knee. Then, slips his hand up a few inches, to give her opportunity to signal him if she wants him to stop. Jillian is almost astonished at this. And delighted. Many kisses. A few inches more. He stops. More kisses, more inches. She's never had this! Every step being coordinated between them, every intimacy implicitly agreed to or available for veto. They hug and kiss, for a long while. William waits for her to fully come down from her earlier turmoil. Jillian is relieved at the pace of things, and William's attentiveness to their moodstates / mindstates. Jillian does not push away or remove his hand. She relaxes her legs.

They kiss again, and William resumes sliding his hand very slowly further up her skirt, with pauses. He enjoys playing with her inner thighs and is aware of her rising pleasure. She relaxes her legs slightly more. He stops just short and pleasure-teases her with his attentions very high up on her thigh and again stops just short. When he hears and feels her breathing a certain way, he presses his hand against his final destination. Jillian gasps! She is astonished at her reaction. Outright astonished! And delighted. William looks at her, pleased. Jillian is pleased with herself too. A warmth suffuses them. Jillian is also mildly embarrassed about having a vocal reaction. Never had that before. Not even close.)

WILLIAM Tell me.

JILLIAN I'm afraid to.

WILLIAM That's our deal. You have to.

JILLIAN I'm afraid you'll take advantage of me.

WILLIAM What! Me?

JILLIAN I know; I'm confusing. I'm confused.

WILLIAM No you're not. Well, you are, but not for long. You're getting unconfused.

JILLIAN I'm feeling ...you've started to make me feel ...that things should have been so different in the past. I'm sad about my past. (Voice becomes very soft) It should have been so different.

WILLIAM (Hugs her) Be quiet for now. I know how long it takes me to fully reveal. Meanwhile, I want to kiss you more, and have you open your legs.

(Shocked at his boldness Jillian giggles, his saying outright what might have taken place anyway. She is, nevertheless, pleased to comply. And is rewarded.)

ACT I

SCENE 6

After a movie, and a drink, talking and walking back to her place.

(On the sofa. More talk about the movie, their families, some history, then kissing. Their making out goes well. Jillian recognizes that her passion level and pleasure level is greater than ever before. As he is pleasing her with his hand and finger, she goes to reciprocate. She is rubbing him. William senses a 'let-me-pleasure-him-to-even-things-out' feeling rather than Jillian's own moment-to-moment pleasure in following his body cues. He stops her.)

JILLIAN Why are you stopping me?

WILLIAM Jillian, sweetie, I'm so happy with what you were doing and where it might have gone, but something is wrong.

JILLIAN What? Was I doing it wrong?

WILLIAM Yes. You weren't fully in the moment with me. I want you to follow *my* body cues like I do yours. I didn't feel *only* pleasure on your part. ...I felt hurry or obligation. Something like that. I want you to take only pleasure in me. *Intense* pleasure, preferably. (Smiles) Not obligation or hurry.

JILLIAN Oh god, I'm caught again! I'm sorry. I don't know what to say. ...I *did* feel that I wanted to touch you and give you pleasure.

WILLIAM But the way you were doing it, felt rushed. You didn't read me and let my body changes guide you.

JILLIAN You're right, I'm sorry, I did feel a push from my past.

WILLIAM Thank you. I'd love for you to do different things to me, with me, but I don't want your past part of our present.

(They kiss and make out more, and Jillian gets another jolt of unaccustomed pleasure. After....)

JILLIAN William, you make me so crazy, I want you to take all of me. Do more than what you did. Make love to me!

WILLIAM I always make love to you.

JILLIAN No! Fuck me! Right now!

WILLIAM (Heart pounding) Jill, darling, I'm struggling to do this right. I love hearing you say that! I'd love that. It's music to my ears. Not yet. Soon but not yet. You need to know more how you should have been given to. And I want to teach you more about following my body cues.

JILLIAN (Pre-tears in eyes) None of my boyfriends had the slightest interest in teaching me! I was always so frightened that I would do something wrong or not good enough and be embarrassed that I didn't know how to please them.

WILLIAM They were fools! Some guys are such idiots. Pleasure skyrockets for both when the couple is in sync. (Pause) Jillian, you never have to worry about feeling incompetent with me. ...Ours is going to be a slow burn, and I'm going to teach you.

ACT I

SCENE 7

After going to a comedy club and stopping off for a drink, they are in the alcove at the end of her hallway.

(Jillian feels her lightweight spring coat slightly open. It tents her. William comes in to kiss her, embracing her back with his left arm, while just before the exact moment that their lips meet, she feels a slight pressure bending her cunthair. They kiss, and she feels the whole of his hand cupping her hair and the base of his middle finger lightly pressing her clitoris. Jillian feels a shock of delight. Oh my god, I'm feeling something through my whole body, from my lips to my cunt. I love the way he makes me feel, I'm almost coming. William pulls away, looks at her, and smiles tenderly. He gives her time for a breath, then kisses her again, this time delaying for a breath before placing his hand and finger again against her cunt and pressing mildly but more insistently. He feels her arousal. He pulls back, looks at her again with his hand still firmly and snugly against her there. Then he releases his hand, kisses her again, and then re-cups and re-presses her cunt, and she gasps and comes. Oh, my god! He lets her breathe. He smiles at her. They embrace again and kiss some more. She feels his hard-on against her, and she reaches around to cup his ass and pulls him into her. And they groove together, until they both come. She loves this. She can't believe he let it happen this way! He smiles. He knows she is thinking that. They kiss a few more times.)

JILLIAN (When she recovers, she laughs) This alcove will never be the same....

ACT I

SCENE 8

Midweek. Jillian and William are finishing another particularly lovely date. Jillian has been so bold as to wear a partly see-through peasant blouse. No bra. They are in the alcove saying goodnight.

(William gently and decisively undoes her coat belt, and her coat falls away to her sides. He looks at her and begins to lean in for a kiss. She feels the bottom of her blouse bend against her ribs. He goes in slowly, but his hands are leading; now she definitely knows he is bringing them up to her breasts. Exactly at the moment they kiss, she feels his hands, both hands, cup her breasts and gently caress them. He pulls back to look at her, hands still cupping and slightly caressing her breasts. He circles her areolas with his index fingers and kisses her. Her nipples respond and harden. A light pinch. Jillian again feels shocked. Oh my god! I just came from my breasts! My cunt is alive too, and he hasn't even touched it! Ohhh, this feels so good.)

JILLIAN (When she recovers, whispers) That was wonderful. Please come in. Don't you want to come in?

WILLIAM (Jillian can tell from his eyes that he would love to come in. He smiles, but pulls back.) Not until I have a good grasp on the elephant in the room.

JILLIAN (Heavy sigh) Oh, no.

WILLIAM Oh, *Yes!* You have to share it with me.

JILLIAN I can't yet. I'm working on it. Working myself up to it.

WILLIAM Then not until you're ready. Until then, I won't come in. We'll play and enjoy each other up to a point here. Where it's limited.

JILLIAN You are a mystery to me. I've never had a guy like you.

WILLIAM Well, either I'm a mystery or I'm nuts passing up opportunities like this. You decide.

JILLIAN You're not nuts. I never imagined it could be like this.

WILLIAM What "this?"

JILLIAN That a guy could want me like you do and not push me for more beyond what I'm ready for. Insisting that I read you like you do me. You slow things down, and I love that.

WILLIAM Right! (Big smile) That's exactly right! That's what I want. Not a hint of forced, not even of self-forced. (Change of voice to playful) Then I'll have your full, unbridled, raunchy and raucous passion, which is how I want you to be with me.

JILLIAN (Smiles) "Raucous." You said that in our first conversation.

WILLIAM (Smiles) I know. But don't change the subject. It's only because of that —mind syncing— that you should be giving.

JILLIAN (Happy, uncertain, processing) Kiss?

WILLIAM (Kiss good night. Hugs, more kisses. Jillian relieved, astonished, and happy.)

ACT I

SCENE 9

Next weekend. Just before they leave to go out on their date.

WILLIAM Jillian, I want you to tweak your breast every fifteen minutes.

JILLIAN What! You're kidding me, right? You're being nuts again.

WILLIAM I'm serious.

JILLIAN In public?!

WILLIAM Yes. Every fifteen minutes. (Glances at his wristwatch)

JILLIAN You're getting weird. Maybe you are nuts.

WILLIAM Maybe. You decide.

(They are having a nice time. In a movie theater, Jillian does it once or twice. Then stops. A little while later William looks at her and taps his watch. Jillian is in much conflict. She does it again.

She is not certain why she is complying. They are outdoors now at a cafe, having a drink. It's been fifteen minutes. William looks at her, then at his left wrist. Jillian is distressed. She is wearing a capelet. She looks at him, and nonchalantly puts her hand under her capelet and draws her fingers down her breast to her nipple. She feels something, very good. They continue to talk. William continues to glance as needed. Jillian goes through her conflict, beginning to enjoy it —being so bold, acknowledging her own desire and growing arousal— but also not liking it because it is outside and what if somebody sees, and a good girl wouldn't do this.

They go home. They make out again in the alcove. This time as they kiss, he slowly drags his hand up her outer thighs. Up and down her thighs. Very slowly, more than once. She feels her miniskirt gathering up each time. She wants more. He wants more. (She whispers in his ear) "I'm near the end of my period. I'm still bleeding a little bit." (He whispers back) "Don't worry about it." She feels his hands slowly circle around to her ass, gently squeezing and cupping her. Also teasing her with his pinky nail. She feels his middle finger slip inside her panties. He plays a little bit, then pulls away and, looking at her, kisses and sucks his finger with its trace of blood. Flabbergasted, Jillian says, "No one...." He says, "You are very special to me," She then kisses his finger. They pause and then resume kissing and playing. She loves it and can't wait. They break and then kiss again, her breath hard. He draws his hand up again, this time in front, reaches her panties, she's sure he will go in now; he doesn't, he drags his index finger along the rim of her panties; she's dying for release. He drags his finger down the side of her panties again feeling the hair of her labia, then up again, her cunthair bristling and folding under his touch. They break. She is really pent now. They kiss again. He reaches up under her skirt again, this time going all the way up bumping into her cunt, and continuing to the top rim of her panties, and then in and down. She feels his finger against her naked cunt. He reads her hardening, sugaring. He feels her breath. She comes. With his eyes he signals her to open her legs. She does. He slips his middle finger inside and enjoys her vagina, sometimes slipping out to circleplay her clitoris. And when she is almost out of breath she comes again, and then again. OMG, she thinks. Never. Never! I can't believe it, and with my period! So much, so many. And I am so wet! Oh god, I feel so good! They break. She feels his cock hard and balls ready to explode. But he pushes away from her. His breath is tense and short.)

JILLIAN Come in.

WILLIAM You don't know how hard it is for me to say No.

JILLIAN Why not?

WILLIAM Because.

JILLIAN Because why?

WILLIAM You complied several times, and that delighted me, but I still saw hesitation and felt your embarrassment.

JILLIAN So, I'm a *normal* woman! And normally a woman wouldn't do that! A *normal* woman.

WILLIAM Well, you're with a non-normal man, if you wish. And *this* non-normal man wants to see you sneaking shows of your desire to provoke him, and hints of your own passion.

JILLIAN I did.

WILLIAM Under duress, some of the time. I want it fully and boldly acknowledged. I watch out for you. You must know that I watch out for you. And, as you saw, it can be done successfully.

JILLIAN You are stubborn.

WILLIAM And you are the beneficiary of my discipline.

JILLIAN (Long pause) Make me come again?

WILLIAM (Big smile. Festivities. She does. Happy.)

WILLIAM (After she, and he, recover.) Goodnight.

JILLIAN No, Come in!

WILLIAM No. We're almost there.

JILLIAN (In an urgent whisper) Come inside. Please, I want to blow you.

WILLIAM (Heart pounding) Jillie ...give *me* a break. I'd love that! Please, we're almost there. No, not yet!

JILLIAN (Disappointment, astonishment, mild anger, curiosity) You are one *very* interesting man! You confuse the hell out of me.

WILLIAM Creatively confuse. ...You're growing, and that gives me a terrible and terribly lovely hardon.

(Smiles and gives her a big hug) I love you. I won't be able to sleep tonight without thinking of you. You know that. I do really love you. We'd better stop talking. Good night. (And leaves, propelling himself away)

ACT II

(The Expansion)

SCENE 1

One week later. They have a great time again. Sharing, laughing, each feeling good about having met someone they like and trust. At the end of the evening, they are in the alcove at the end of her hallway.

WILLIAM When we say goodnight like this, I want you to stand with your legs slightly apart. Anticipating me. Inviting me. Torturing me.

(Jillian feels two things again: stunned and offended almost, at being so boldly told what to do and very excited about what is going to happen. She does. And is rewarded, magnificently. After ....)

JILLIAN Come in now. Please don't be ridiculous.

WILLIAM I'd love to.

JILLIAN Whew! It's been a long time.

(Inside her apartment, sipping cordials.)

Now, it's time for you to reveal to me. Honestly.

WILLIAM ...and you with me.

JILLIAN Why did you have me drag my fingers down my breast every fifteen minutes? Why did you ask me to do that?

WILLIAM Because you have no idea how many times I fantasize about you in just a five-minute span. I want to kiss you and feel you and fuck you and discover all of you.

JILLIAN So?

WILLIAM So ...you're just beginning to let yourself feel your desirability. You don't let yourself acknowledge how desirable you are.

JILLIAN I know I'm cute and that I'm a nice person.

WILLIAM You really have no idea. You're too modest this way. It's not modesty, actually. It's false modesty, or enforced modesty. That's it, enforced modesty. You minimize your self-worth. For you, "good" means being self-effacing. Being non-assertive. And certainly not self-affirming.

JILLIAN What's wrong with being modest? I like being modest. If more people were, the world would be a nicer place.

WILLIAM I agree with you about that, but I'm talking about you being unwilling to acknowledge something positive. Something objectively true. How desirable you are. You wrap yourself in a cloak of "modesty" because ...something ...I don't have it yet. And it's connected to your sexual energy ...you block a lot of it.

JILLIAN (Not believing it, but processing) And by making me tweak my breast?

WILLIAM I want you to tease me, blatantly tease me. You won't let yourself acknowledge how desirable you are. I want you to be confident of your desirability. And I want you to be aware of your desires. I want you to *actively* torment me with shows of your sensuality. I want to see both your self-confidence and your awareness of your desirability, your sexiness.

JILLIAN (Uncertain)

WILLIAM And *not* just a little bit, and *not* just now and then. And, I want you to have *fantasies* about me, and to tell me about them, and to signal me of your desires, and to act on them. All that. I want you to provoke me with your confidence!

JILLIAN That's a lot of "wants."

WILLIAM You bet. And if you don't like being so wanted, you have the wrong guy.

JILLIAN What if I told you to do something similar?

WILLIAM That's ridiculous! I'd do it if you requested me to ...if that would turn you on ...if that would make you almost wet, like your doing it makes me ...I'd do it. ...I'll do it right now if you'd like. Gladly. What would you like?

JILLIAN No!...We were talking about you.

WILLIAM Actually ...we were talking about you. How I want you to torment me with your sensuality. Then I reassured you that I would fulfill any sexual request of yours, but I don't need to, not at his moment anyway.

JILLIAN Why?

WILLIAM Because I'm so turned on by you. I fantasize about you incessantly.

JILLIAN That's a fine word, "incessantly." How much is that? And why should I do that anyway?

WILLIAM In *five* minutes, I think about you sexually three hundred times. As for the other question, I've already told you, I want to see your desires —for me— and I want to see you *feeling* them. I want you to be confident and to acknowledge them boldly. Blatantly.

JILLIAN Wow! Are you kidding me? Me? Even while we're talking? (Little laugh) I have to process this. No one has talked to me like this before. This is a little hard to believe.

WILLIAM You. Yes. I have two movies running at the same time: everything else, and sex with you.

JILLIAN Then why do you leave me abruptly. How can you leave like you do when we say goodnight? In the state you are in? You give me orgasms and make me crazy. I've never had anything like it! But you won't come into my place and let me pleasure you? Why not? How do you stand it?

WILLIAM Sit down. (Smiles)

JILLIAN We are sitting! (Laughs, realizes that he knew that)

WILLIAM (Smiles) I know. ...Jill, something in you needed repair. ...You weren't ready.

JILLIAN (First reaction goes toward offended) Come on! I'm not a virgin. I've done things with other guys.

WILLIAM Right! And you *shouldn't* have. I mean, not before you were convinced that they were really into you. You should have *required* better experiences *before* you did those things. They had to earn those things.

(Pause, debating)

And *they* should have given you more. Something was wrong with *them*! They should have wanted to! They should have *wanted* to give you more, a *lot* more. ...And you should have *required* it!

JILLIAN Uh oh, I'm feeling it again.

WILLIAM What?

JILLIAN What I told you ...that evening, after the concert.

WILLIAM Right. He especially damaged you. Your self-confidence was injured; instead of growing from your experiences, it was stunted. Even now you don't admit how much he injured you.

Right from the start the fears you had —that you've told me about— ran in the background. Fogged you. And he sensed them. And he didn't care. He took advantage of them, your self-doubts and your family situation. He cracked the whip, and you complied.

(Pauses to assess)

Worse, then you *internalized* less-than-reciprocal-giving as standard. You made it "all right," because, 'What can you expect?'

...The damage he inflicted on you, *imprinted* on you, and what you then *self*-expected, has had a lasting effect.

...Until me. (Big smile) You're changing and have changed, but you don't fully realize it even now.

JILLIAN (Silent)

WILLIAM I've thought a lot about our talks, what you shared and confessed. I told you I would think about it, and I have my answer. You have not been rightly given to by your previous boyfriends. I know this from what you've confessed directly, but I suspected it even before that when you had your "blips" and lost sync with me. I felt your mind-body, if I may use that term. I have antennae that way; I'm fully with the girl or woman I'm with and at the same time I'm fully with myself.

JILLIAN (Mixed emotions) I'll ask you more about *that* some other time, but now answer my other question.

WILLIAM (Purposely stalling and letting her see it) "Other," "other," I'm confused. Too many "others." Which question? I forget.

JILLIAN (Just looks at him)

WILLIAM (Let's a smile grow) Before I answer that, I need you to know something.

JILLIAN What?

WILLIAM You're going to have a hard time believing this. You are very different than a lot of women, Jill.

JILLIAN Oh come on! I'm just like a lot of women. ...What makes me so different?

WILLIAM Your openness. Your capacity to trust. And your basic honesty and decency.

JILLIAN Okay, so....

WILLIAM And you're not grasping, materialistic or manipulative.

JILLIAN That's all very nice. But that's so special?

WILLIAM Yes. You don't even realize it. And you're steady and low-maintenance. Not a drama queen.

JILLIAN This is all lovely and I thank you for seeing me this way. But you haven't answered my question. It's still hanging, and you don't want me to feel that you've told me all this to soften me up.

WILLIAM (Smiles) Right.

After I leave you, Jill, I usually go home and think about our evening. I think about it, in *micro*-detail. I replay it down to your breath-changes as we were playing. I think about you and what I did and how you reacted, and where I know I can take you to. I fantasize about how much I can grow you; sexually, emotionally and intellectually.

JILLIAN (Smiles, gestures with hands, Go on.)

WILLIAM. And I masturbate about it.

JILLIAN Oh my god! (Giggles, pleased, and slightly embarrassed for him) You! Do? ...About me?

WILLIAM Yes. About *you*. And us, if we continue to grow as an "item." A couple.

JILLIAN There's no "if," as far as I'm concerned. ...But why haven't you enjoyed me fully? And let me enjoy you fully?

WILLIAM There is an answer to that. A non-nuts answer.

(Locks eyes with her) ...It would have been rushing things.

(Assessing) I wanted you badly, but not for the long run, the way I found you. I felt you as an insecure kitten whose fur was all matted, and I knew I could grow you into the regal Siamese you are becoming. (She smiles, he smiles back)

You are not *like* other women, many of them, anyway, so I don't treat you like other women. Many believe that sex is required, and promptly! Some expect it and even want it that way. They think it proves their desirability. Or their "equality." Some think that if they don't offer it or if the guy doesn't push for it right away —oral or vagina-penis— that it means that they're not desired, or something is wrong with him.

JILLIAN (Smiles, then pensive) Okay, you're more of an expert on this subject than me. ...You really have thought a lot about this. I don't think most guys do.

WILLIAM A lot of people don't think about a lot of things. I do.

Unless I gave to you that way —the way you should have been given to and should have required— you would not have *felt* it, the way you needed to feel it, from your body up to your mind. From *felt* experience. I *wanted* to give that to you when we were together. And want to, all the time. (Pauses, assesses)

Only now that you're metabolizing my love and the *way* I make love to you, have you started to believe that you deserve it. And deserved it. Undeniably. If I had let you rush into full sex —which I might have if I didn't feel you as different, and if I hadn't felt that you had to be healed to restart you growing— we wouldn't be where we are now.

JILLIAN (Audibly huffs) ...Wow. You give me a lot to think about. (Long pause) Thank you, for all that. I love you for all that.

(Very long pause, assessing) And not, "usually?"

WILLIAM Not usually?

JILLIAN You said before that usually you go home and think about me. "Usually."

WILLIAM (Nods in acknowledgment, body tenses, gathers himself, releases.) Jillian, I want you to hear me out before reacting. Can you do that?

JILLIAN I'll try.

WILLIAM ...I have two special friends that I see from time to time.

JILLIAN What! Wait a minute! Friends? ...What do you mean, "friends?" And where do you "see" them? ...And how does that explain how you can leave me in your condition?

WILLIAM (Nods) Two friends. Roberta, and her sister, Caitlin. One apartment. They live about two, three miles away.

JILLIAN Oh, great! And how do you know Roberta, and Caitlin, and how *friendly* are you?

WILLIAM Okay, slow down. Roberta, I've known for four years. We have a great bond. Intellectually and emotionally. She and I are like sister and brother that way. ...We were also lovers.

JILLIAN *"Were."* ...And Caitlin?

WILLIAM I've known Caitlin about a year and a half, since she moved in temporarily with Roberta.

JILLIAN I *knew* it! (Deflated) You don't know how this hurts me! How could you? I don't get it! I have trusted you so much.... I'm letting you explore me and teach me things, and meanwhile you have other women?

WILLIAM I don't "have" other women. Jillian, please hear me out. My relationship with them has been ongoing but as I've been gravitating more and more into orbit with you, my relationship with them has been changing. And it *isn't* what you think in the first place.

Your trust is *the* most important thing. We were in the earliest stage of getting to know each other. And there were issues —the ones we're discussing— that we had to resolve.

JILLIAN So what happens after our dates and you go over there? The *truth*!

WILLIAM If I know they'll be home, I may go over. We talk. Mainly talk. It depends. (Bracing himself) There were three occasions when Roberta or Caitlin and I made love.

JILLIAN What?! When you leave me you go over there you make love to them, you fuck them?

WILLIAM No.

JILLIAN That's what you just *said!*

WILLIAM No. I sometimes did after dates, with other girls. Women. But it's much more than that. It's complex, please don't prejudge it just yet. I simply enjoy them more, especially Roberta. Their personalities.

JILLIAN (Disbelief, combined with anger) …And the other one, Caitlin?

WILLIAM "The other one, Caitlin," what?

JILLIAN What do you do? Did. The last time you did it. I want to know. I need to know.

WILLIAM Sit down.

JILLIAN We *are* sitting.

WILLIAM I *know*. (Pause) I'm giving you all this ...I'm letting you squeeze me this way ...do you know why?

JILLIAN No. Why?

WILLIAM First, because you trusted me enough to let me ask you things. And you answered them honestly. Reluctantly —and not completely, at first— but honestly. Things you *hated* to tell me.

JILLIAN (Looks away)

WILLIAM Jill, I *hated* to hear them. Believe me, I *still* smart from them when I image them.

JILLIAN (Still looks away)

WILLIAM And, second, because I want you to know *me* that well. We won't work if you don't. I'm letting myself be vulnerable to you. Intimacy squared. Is that bad?

JILLIAN No, that's good. Thank you, I think. God you are so *different!* (Pause) But I still want the answer to my question.

WILLIAM (Obvious feint, small smile) What question?

JILLIAN (Just looks at him)

WILLIAM With Roberta, it was the evening of the day you and I colored the Easter eggs.

JILLIAN And with Caitlin?

WILLIAM The last time was after I met you at the bar.

JILLIAN What did you do that night?

WILLIAM We made love. But that was not the *point* of the encounter. It was much more than that.

JILLIAN (Thinking, *How could you?*)

WILLIAM (Sensing crush, stops talking)

JILLIAN (Further plunge)

WILLIAM I liked you. I was interested. We had just had our first date.

JILLIAN (She mouths, *What?* but no words come out.)

WILLIAM I really liked you, but we were not "an item" yet, or even close. So unproven.

JILLIAN (Breathing hard, partially recovered) And how often have you been with her since then?

WILLIAM None, physically.

JILLIAN None? We've been going out more than three months and you just went cold turkey, really?

WILLIAM Yes. No. I've seen them and talked with them, but Yes, it's not been physical if you don't count hugs and kisses. Cheek kisses. And we mainly talk.

(Knowing she needs more.) After I started dating you I told Roberta, and Caitlin, about how I was starting to feel about you. My comfort with you and my enjoyment of you. And how you respond to me, and have let me open your mind, and that you've trusted me enough to reveal your past. And my intuitions about where I could bring you and where we could go as a couple.

Roberta quipped that I was, "dangerously close," to becoming serious about you. (Glances quickly at her) That was a joke; she knows how I am.

JILLIAN (Flashes an angry, 'I don't need an explanation' look!) I know too. And that was the last time?

WILLIAM Yes ...with one exception.

JILLIAN What?

WILLIAM We did other things.

JILLIAN She blew you.

WILLIAM Yes....

JILLIAN She blew you and you brought her off.

WILLIAM Yes. (Quickly adding, to prevent her from going where he knew it would go.) Jill, I've had to withstand your answers to my questions, and I hated what I heard. But that you confessed to me I love, and love you for it, but I hated what I heard, nevertheless. What you're hearing —what we're talking about— Is different. Very different. It, the sex part, is in the context of mutually giving and loving relationships.

JILLIAN (Ignoring) She blew you ...*and you let her!*

WILLIAM We shared more about what really shaped us into who we are. The arc of our development. The deepest stuff. We had had a particularly intense night of soul-sharing. As we're doing right now ...as I'm doing with you right now.

(Earnestly, but trying not to sound defensive) ...I'm telling you, our honesty level drives the sexual part. It's a natural expression. We cherish that. Our relationship is night-and-day different from your first relationship and next few experiences.

(Jillian tearing up, William reading her) We're at that level, too. You and I will have that. You'll see, if you continue with me.

JILLIAN You can stop saying that. I'm working on things. You want that, don't you? So stop saying that!

WILLIAM I'm sorry. I was being defensive. I really love what we have, and I don't want to lose you.

(Reaches to hug her. Jillian allows it.)

Roberta's convinced I'm smitten with you. ...And if I can tell you something and have you believe it....

JILLIAN Yes....

WILLIAM She said this might be the last time we can do this. She knew that I'm in love with you, and I acknowledged both.

JILLIAN Thank you. Good. Okay, I get that you two really have a connection, but this still sounds like a horny dog story to me. You have the best of both worlds.

WILLIAM (Interrupting) Jillie, please, this isn't a "Let me fuck you," or a "Suck me off" story.

JILLIAN Sure, sure. Then what *is* it?

WILLIAM *Are* you *listening*? I am so grateful for her understanding me, for the simple, deep back–and–forth that we have. She knows who I am, and loves me for being who I am.

JILLIAN I do too! But I've never heard anything like this! Or even read about anything like this! This is so hard to believe and understand. I want to believe you, but this *is* hard to believe.

WILLIAM I know. It's very different, but that doesn't matter. This isn't a fuckstory. We love and respect each other and have great communication and understanding. *That's* what starts me a hardon with her.

JILLIAN (Sarcastic) Oh, and not her mouth!

WILLIAM Jill, don't be snide. If it were just that, this would be a whole different story, and I would not feel about her the way I do. And I'm never snide or hurtful to you. I endure your stories, even though they're painful for me to hear. I could have said things that would have hurt you if I just reacted from my primitive brain. I could have. I've never wanted to. I always try to understand what you shared with me, confessed to me, from the inside of your experience. Your motivation. How you saw yourself and your world at the time. ...Do the same for me. Make the effort from your heart.

JILLIAN I am trying to. It's so hard. Your whole story is so different. Your whole way of being.

WILLIAM "*Hard*?" ...You think it's "hard?" ...When I image what you've confessed to me, and I do, in detail —in as much detail as you've permitted me to know— I have to use all my fairness to antidote my reactions. I tell myself, 'She had her reasons,' 'I wasn't there,' and, 'I couldn't have been.'

Let me tell you something, a fantasy of mine. I imagine that if I ever meet him, you know who, say at a high school reunion of yours, I'd knee him in the nuts. And if his wife is with him, all the better. When she screams, "Why did you do that!" I'd turn to her and say, calmly, "Ask your husband," and then I'd turn away.

But I'd turn back and add, "No, he'd likely lie or not even remember. He raped Jillian, for your information. A 'soft' rape as rapes go, but a rape, nonetheless. Ask him for the pungent details."

JILLIAN (Breath short) Okay, I get it. I'll work on it ...to put you into perspective from the inside of your experience.

WILLIAM Thank you.

JILLIAN But, if you think I'm different, I'm only a little different maybe; you're off-the-charts!

WILLIAM Well, off or on, that's me, and I'm making myself as open and vulnerable to you as I've insisted you be with me.

JILLIAN (Sighs hard) I know. I'm trying to understand, but it still hurts.

WILLIAM Jill, I make myself process images that I can't *stand* to image. I try to feel your essence at that time. Your needs. Why what happened, happened. The context of your life, including your family, and what was happening culturally at the time.

JILLIAN I know you do. I appreciate that you listen to me that way. ...It's just that it's weird.

WILLIAM Please. Stop that! ...Don't use that word for this. I don't like when you talk sloppy. "Weird" is too all-inclusive. It's vague and condemnatory.

Think about what I'm telling you. "Unusual," it is, but "weird," it's not. ...Unless you truly think I'm "weird." But if so, why be with me?

JILLIAN I don't know.

WILLIAM Am I not proving out?

JILLIAN I'm thinking, What would anybody else think of this?

WILLIAM Oh! So *that's* what you're thinking! You're afraid someone else would judge you for not freaking out on me. No one else's opinion matters. If I'm giving and getting love, that's the end of the story. No one is being stolen from or deprived or abused or diminished. You have evidence from your own experience with me.

JILLIAN It's just

WILLIAM It's *"just"* very different then your experience, so I'd appreciate it if you would stop thinking about it in a preformed way and then labeling it with words that don't apply.

JILLIAN How would *any* woman think about it!

WILLIAM Not "any" woman. The common denominator is not what I'm going for, with *you*. *And*, I can name two that don't, and a third —you, I hope— who will not use "any" woman as her standard of reference.

JILLIAN You're making me think ...but I still feel hurt.

WILLIAM Jillian, did your boyfriends —especially one whose name I will not use —ever work to please you, to make you c—

JILLIAN *Stop* William! You know the answer to that. No.

WILLIAM You know where I was going with that. But even *more* importantly —and you *will* listen to this— did he really want to know your essence? To develop you to your highest level?

JILLIAN You know the answer to that too.

WILLIAM Did any of them?

JILLIAN No. Not really.

WILLIAM Then I demand that you consider my relationships, both with them and with you, on that basis. Not on the basis of other peoples' "morality;" so-called morality. That's their movie. Someone else's movie. I love you and want you to be the best you can be and, I am letting you have access to my soul. My mind's cunt. What's more moral and beautiful than that?

(Pause) ...And, how many guys would do that?

JILLIAN None. ...Okay, ...Okay, I'll try to consider it that way. I need time, though.

WILLIAM Thank you, I appreciate it. That's partly why I love you.

ACT II

SCENE 2

At Jillian's apartment after a, 'We have to talk,' telephone call.

WILLIAM Hello.

JILLIAN Hello, William. (Pregnant pause)

WILLIAM So....?

JILLIAN So....

WILLIAM To cut to the chase ...is it over?

JILLIAN I didn't say that. Not necessarily. Don't jump the gun. I want you to tell me more about your relationships with them. It's the only way I can possibly trust you. I need more depth and detail.

WILLIAM I'll be as totally honest as you've been with me. I need your trust in me. I'm not going to lie to you nor go behind your back. ...I've resigned myself to fate; you will love me for who I am, or you won't.

JILLIAN (Withholds a response)

WILLIAM I'll start, so that you don't have to grill me.

JILLIAN Good! I don't want to feel "like I'm a dentist extracting teeth." (Both smile at the echo, but the tension overrules laughter.)

WILLIAM When I met Roberta, I knew from the start that she was different from any other woman I had ever known. I have never met anybody —woman or man, even David— with whom my mind and personality more easily syncs. She was integrated both sexually and emotionally. We resonated. Roberta was the first person in my life who accepted me fully for who I am. Never tried to make me feel guilty for being me. I grew to appreciate her more and more, and loved her, and eventually fell in love with her, and she with me. We've had great sex and great sharing, and I can't imagine ever not loving each other. She is very dear to me, but I am not *in* love with her now.

JILLIAN What changed?

WILLIAM After Roberta and I had been with each other for some time, I was plagued by the gnawing feeling that I owed it to our honesty level to admit to her that I would always need *some* extra experiences. I wrestled with not mentioning it but that would have put our relationship on a lie-basis. We wanted it on a truth-basis. I was thoroughly satisfied with her, that was not in question, but I knew I would need that, eventually. I braced for the worst.

JILLIAN Okay... That's *another* bombshell! We need to talk about that, but for now, go on....

WILLIAM I told her, "not many and not often, but not never."

JILLIAN What did she say to that?

WILLIAM She was quiet for a very long time. Finally, she held my eyes and said, "I can handle that."

Then, after another very long time she said, "If I give you that freedom, I want it too. *If* I want it. I'm not saying I *would*, but, you know ...the goose and the gander."

We talked a lot about it. A lot. Double standard and all that. Is it fair? But in the end, double standard didn't matter. I would not allow it. I said No.

Weeks later, I asked her *how* she would be able to "handle it." She said, "I think men are more insecure that way. To a large extent, 'anatomy *is* destiny.' Psychology can harness biology and override it to an extent, temporarily, but basically women know that they are desired, at least for sex. Most of them, most of the time. Think about it: if a woman wants it and is determined to get laid on a given night, all she has to do is go someplace, a bar or shopping, and allow herself to get picked up. But a guy, even if he really wants it, has no guarantee it will happen. Men, males, more often need to prove something to themselves." I think she's right.

But there's another factor and that one's even *more* important. For me. My apex thrill is if I can bring a girl —a special woman— to the point of unconflicted exuberance about her sexuality and me. I enjoy *growing* a girl or woman. For me it's not the number of notches.

JILLIAN So then what changed with you and this wonderful lover?

WILLIAM Nothing had to change. We talked about marriage but decided not to. Mainly me, but also her.

JILLIAN Why not?

WILLIAM Ultimately ...because we are too similar.

JILLIAN What does that mean?

WILLIAM She is as independent as me. She wanted my consent, hypothetically, and I said No. So, even though she's okay with me having other experiences once in a long while and I would be from the bottom of my heart profoundly grateful to her for that, it couldn't work for me reciprocally. This one aspect of our similarity cuts across the grain of my identity and personality. And maybe masculine pride too. It's too important. So, No.

We still loved each other, including physically sometimes, but we both agreed that it would be better to also see other people. Until we met someone important for the future. We dated some. She had two short-term "things" and I had one, but neither of us had anything significant. ...Until you. ...My "significant other." (Smiles)

JILLIAN (Taking all that in but straining to not lose her focus.) And so how does Caitlin come into the picture I'm afraid to ask?

WILLIAM Caitlin had been dating someone. After they broke off, she eventually confided to her sister that she inconsistently orgasmed. That wasn't the reason for the breakup, but she wanted to talk to someone. She naturally thought that Roberta might help her by saying something, pointing her in a direction. They talked a lot about it.

JILLIAN Oh *no*! You're torturing me. You *know* what I'm thinking.

WILLIAM Yes. Right. Roberta suggested to Caitlin that she let me teach her.

JILLIAN She did! I can't believe this! Between sisters? And you did?

WILLIAM Yes.

JILLIAN Oh, and I am sure you did it only as a public service of course. (Bitterly) And I am also sure she was a good student and is very grateful to you no doubt? Boy, this is a lot to process! Wow.

WILLIAM Please keep this in context. I am not a gigolo. Her time with me, our time together, was more like Improvisation classes and psychotherapy sessions than anything else.

JILLIAN Uh huh, "sessions." ...With a dollop of sex! (Tears up) Do you love them?

WILLIAM Yes.

JILLIAN Both?

WILLIAM Yes.

JILLIAN (Starting to cry) What are you *telling* me? Are you *in* love with them?

WILLIAM No. I've told you.

JILLIAN Tell me again. Please tell me the truth!

WILLIAM I've told you and will tell you again and again, I love you and I am not *in* love with either of them. And that's the truth, and I will only tell you the truth!

JILLIAN (Big sigh) I almost wish you hadn't told me all of this. Most men wouldn't have. Probably. Not completely.

(Pause, fear and anger resurging)

So ...you're not in love with Caitlin, even though she fucks you and sucks you?

WILLIAM She doesn't *do* that, but if you put it that way, then Yes.

JILLIAN How *should* I put it! How do *you* put it?

WILLIAM How I put it is that I've had the privilege of teaching her about her body and herself. Yes, I've enjoyed her body and her mind, and she mine; but I feel it....

JILLIAN Come on! (Frowning) You're telling me a fairy tale! You want me to believe in fairy tales now, do you?

WILLIAM It's how I feel. Call it what you wish.

JILLIAN You're not in love with her?

WILLIAM I feel very tenderly towards her. I do love her, as a person, but I am not in love with her. I grew her. That was the apex thrill for me.

JILLIAN "Was" ...you mean it?

WILLIAM Yes.

JILLIAN And, you really *feel* it that way?

WILLIAM (Just looks at her)

JILLIAN (Trying to process it all, but unable to let go of the physical part) ...So, let me get this straight... after our dates you go over there, and you talk and share and play, and one or the other fucks you or sucks you off, (purposely making it worse for herself) or both. "Depending."

WILLIAM It's *not* how you keep imagining it. It's not my boutique brothel. Broaden your imagination! ...And No, it was never *a trois.*

JILLIAN Why not? Some men fantasize that. You may have.

WILLIAM. Certain things should be sacred. I've told you that. I never wanted to mix our separate experiences. I might enjoy the type of playtime you're suggesting but I've never fantasized about it with them. What we do or did is sacred to me.

JILLIAN Could you have sex with them now, while dating me?

WILLIAM You know, you keep putting it *wrongly*! I never went over there for sex.

Jillian, you are the first woman that's come into my life that I feel I want to grow with. In years. And keep growing with. I feel a different kind of happiness with you. I love it.

You are central.

(Long silence) Let's walk over to the river. We need a cool breeze.

JILLIAN (On Riverside Park walkway) How am I different from Roberta?

WILLIAM I can be long-winded about that, but in a nutshell, it's your beat. Your essential timing.

JILLIAN More. ...That's not enough.

WILLIAM You're both women and a little more quickly emotional than me, but you are more patient than her, and you operate in a different intellectual-emotional key. (Long pause)

...And if you're making comparisons sexually, don't. Please don't. I never compare you, even in the privacy of my mind. Whenever I am with you, I am completely with you. You can tell that from how I am with you.

JILLIAN (Just breathes hard, then wraps her arms around him.)

ACT II

SCENE 3

A few days later, after dinner, at William's apartment.

JILLIAN William, I need to know some more details about you, and Roberta and Caitlin.

WILLIAM It's my time in the tank again? Okay, dunk me.

JILLIAN When you and Roberta agreed to start seeing other people, how did you work out being intimate with them? But before you begin your confessions, I want you to clarify something. The night we met, you were with Roberta later?

WILLIAM Wow! For you to have confused this, it must have really rattled you! It was Caitlin. And it was not for relief.

JILLIAN It rattles me all right! I'm trying to understand it and trying to accept it in your terms, but you have to admit it's way out of the ordinary. Way out.

And Roberta? Why haven't you made love with her again?

WILLIAM I found myself unexpectedly more and more interested in you. I enjoy being with you, our increasing bond, and how you respond to me. I dig you.

And she has had dates of her own, naturally.

JILLIAN Unexpectedly?

WILLIAM You know, dating often turns South the more you get to know someone well. But that wasn't the case with you. I found you, find you, increasingly interesting.

JILLIAN (Allowing the conversation to turn) What makes me so interesting?

WILLIAM Your smile at first, and your legs, as I've told you, but more and more, your personality.

JILLIAN (Ignoring) So what's the deal, the arrangement?

WILLIAM You must know something. I put restrictions on us.

JILLIAN *What!* What kind of "restrictions?" And don't dawdle! No roundabout storyframing please.

WILLIAM (Delays. Inhales. Holds eye contact.) She could not blow me if that had happened within the last week and we couldn't fuck if she had happened to have done that within half a week.

JILLIAN (Staggered. When recovers) And how did you come up with those figures: a week, and half a week?

WILLIAM The first is twice as intimate than the other, I feel.

JILLIAN It sounds a bit ridiculous, waiting a few days or one week.

WILLIAM No, not ridiculous at all. I needed her, both of them, to feel clean for me. *I* want it that way. To not have recent memory or taste of another man when with me. I also wanted to feel clean for *them*.

I didn't have anywhere near as much "good luck" as you may think, so I didn't often have a lot to "track" that way, and neither did she, although she had more "luck" than me.

(Light but urgent tone) My insistence was a way of sacramentalizing what might happen on a given occasion. Abstinence as purification. It may not have much biological significance but emotionally it's very meaningful for me. And then, it became so for all of us. I wanted us, on any potential occasion, to come to each other clean. (Smiles) Like vestal virgins. Bathed, and wearing white. Cleansed. Sanctified.

Introibo ad altare dei.

And please remember who dreamed this up! ...Hint: it was a guy. ...This guy.

JILLIAN I get it. As much as I wish none of this came with you, I respect what you just said. I like you for that.

What if she were getting serious with a boyfriend?

WILLIAM I would have to cross that bridge at that time. She would let me know. And I've already crossed certain emotional bridges and I'm sure she's worked on herself similarly. We're not *in* love now although what we have in the way of love and respect for each other exceeds most marriages.

(A long pause) Jill, I'd like a cold drink. How about an iced tea?

(He goes to the kitchen and gets two drinks)

JILLIAN ...Everything about you is so different than anything I've known or even heard about. ...Even how you think and talk.

WILLIAM Well, ...then judge me by who I am. My combination of assets and, if you wish to call it something, my "idiosyncrasy." Don't judge me by Society's one-size-fits-all fiats. Fuck society's fiats! In this realm I can decide for myself and so can you.

You have to know me for who I am. This is as much a part of me as how I think and speak. If you can't accept me, then it's better to end it sooner rather than later. I am not going to have another disaster in my life if it can be avoided. I don't want to lose you and what we have, but....

JILLIAN William, honey, stop jumping the gun. I'm also working on some very hard questions. I'm trying to guesstimate, 'Can I trust him, long-term?' and, 'How do I know he won't just dump me at some future point?' *And*, 'Can I handle this about you, do I even want to?' You would have these questions too if you were a woman.

WILLIAM Please, listen. I'm giving you my soul. My "saucerful of secrets." I've opened myself up to you, equivalent to what you did to me. If my level of sharing back isn't the ultimate proof of my being a loving partner, then I don't know what is.

We will work out. I have no doubt of it.

JILLIAN (Heavy sigh) I hear you and I want us to work out. I am taking in all that you've said. Give me time.

WILLIAM (Goes to her, hugs her and says softly to her) Thank you, I appreciate your willingness to consider and reconsider. That is a very unusual and wonderful quality.

(Tightens the hug and whispers in her ear)

You know, sometimes when we're on the phone, my balls crinkle up.

JILLIAN (Giggles. Smiling.) They do?

WILLIAM Yes. Hearing your voice gets me started. And knowing that I can have your mind. That you are willing to share your whole soul with me. Even the parts that no one knows or will ever know. That I can have access to your mind's cunt. ...And that no one else can.

JILLIAN Ohhh I like that! ...I'm even a little excited although I don't know how *that* can be, given what we're talking about.

WILLIAM It's our level of trust.

JILLIAN You're amazing. (Recovering) Or maybe nuts! ...I'm not sure which.

WILLIAM Yup. One of the two. You decide. (Smiles)

JILLIAN Oh, I'm dying here. That you're so honest with me I love, and I die of jealousy listening to you.

WILLIAM That's exactly how *I* felt, listening to *you*.

JILLIAN (Gathers herself) I know, but I was in one-on-one relationships. I never had other guys at the same time.

WILLIAM Oh, so being in a committed relationship with an ape, —a truly emotionally blunted, marginally aware "nice-guy" buffoon— is better? ...Who told you that? Society? I don't think so.

Base your moral judgments on the essence.

JILLIAN (Listening, but not appearing to) ...And that was the last time you saw her and Caitlin?

WILLIAM Back to that? Yes, in the sense you mean.

JILLIAN What other sense is there?

WILLIAM I've seen her and Roberta three other times since we've been dating. "Seen," as in visually. And *talked* with. Roberta twice, alone, and them together, once. They're *friends*.

I think we've had enough. Can we stop? Are you satisfied?

JILLIAN For now.

(William tentatively hugs her, then lengthens it to an unrestrained hug, which she almost matches. He kisses her cheek.)

WILLIAM Shall we go for the walk now?

JILLIAN Yes.

WILLIAM (Later, on the return walk) Would you like to meet them?

JILLIAN No! I don't know. No.

ACT II

SCENE 4

A few weeks later, at Roberta's apartment.

CAITLIN So, when are William and Jillian supposed to be here?

ROBERTA Soon. He's probably looking for a parking spot right now. You know, he circles the block once before putting the car in a garage.

CAITLIN Are you anxious?

ROBERTA No, why should I be? I'm eager to meet her.

CAITLIN Do you think he's told her about us?

ROBERTA Yes.

CAITLIN All about us?

ROBERTA Yes.

CAITLIN Do you think he loves her? I mean, is in love with her?

ROBERTA Yes.

CAITLIN How do you know that?

ROBERTA I just do.

CAITLIN Come on.

ROBERTA (Laughs)

CAITLIN Come on.

ROBERTA I know it because he would never have told her all about us if he didn't love her.

CAITLIN (Laughs)

ROBERTA You know how he is. (Joking) He's a Scorpio; he keeps his secrets.

(Laughs again. Doorbell rings. William and Jillian enter.)

WILLIAM Hi, Caitlin. This is Jillian.

CAITLIN Hi.

JILLIAN Hello.

CAITLIN Come in. Please, come in.

(Roberta walking in from the living room)

ROBERTA (Big warm smile) Hello.

JILLIAN Hello.

ROBERTA I'm so glad to meet you! Let me take your jacket. (Brief small talk) Before we sit down, let me show you the view from the window. On a clear day we can see the Chrysler Building. I love looking at it. (More small talk)

WILLIAM If you haven't prepared anything, I'll just dash around the corner for Chinese and some beer.

ROBERTA Of *course* we've prepared something, Silly! Do you think we're *savages* and don't know how to host your special person and our new friend? (All chuckle)

WILLIAM Right. Of course you have. (Diverting) ...What is it?

CAITLIN Our *specialite´ du maison* (Big smile and gesture) ...paella.

WILLIAM (Smiles back) Great. Then all you need is beer.

ROBERTA (Put off, but with love) William, slow down! When Jillian is comfortable you can go. I know you're trying to encourage us to talk freely —without your influence— but give us a few minutes. *Really*. Let's relax a little first. I've never seen you so edgy.

WILLIAM You're right. You read my mind. (Quick shift, gathering himself) Stop doing that! Jillian will think you're a witch. ...I already know you are. (All chuckle)

ROBERTA (Jokingly over-emphasizing) I am *not*. It's just that you are so *obvious*.

JILLIAN. (Picking the moment to show her strength.) It's all right. I'm fine.

ROBERTA All right then, go "dash."

(Some more small talk, then Roberta shifts to real talk.)

ROBERTA William is quite smitten with you Jillian, and it's sweet for us to see this. ...You should know that he is very particular about women. He screens them carefully.

JILLIAN Well, I don't know how I'm so special as to be, "particular," but I do enjoy and respect him, and he seems to like me.

ROBERTA Jillian, "seems to like you," he's in love with you!

JILLIAN How do you know that?

(Roberta and Caitlin share a glance)

ROBERTA (Big smile) *Aside* from it being obvious, and *aside* from him telling us —'I think I'm falling in love with her'— it's because he never would have told you about us if he didn't trust you. And if he weren't in love with you, he would certainly not have told you *all* about our relationships.

JILLIAN (Blushing) You know all that he has told me?

CAITLIN and ROBERTA Yes.

ROBERTA (Gently) We're his best friends. Us, and David, and Charles. I want this to be a warm first meeting and we both really want you to feel comfortable.

Let me take the lead and address the elephant in the room. I imagine, Jillian, that you've wondered about Caitlin and myself, and the unusualness of our relationship with William.

JILLIAN (Blushing again) Um hmm.

ROBERTA I know. Even on an every-so-often and on-and-off basis, most sisters don't share a lover. ...Actually, I want to retract the word I just used. I said "share" just now, but that's not right. On an accounting basis it might be correct, but it's not really right ...on a soul basis.

JILLIAN Yes, it's very unusual. (Summoning her courage) I've struggled with feeling it weird.

JILLIAN (Looks intently at Roberta, waiting)

ROBERTA I gifted William to Caitlin. In part. In aspects. I wanted my sister to be and to have everything she could have. I knew about her early boyfriends and her mostly lame lovers, and some mistakes she made. And I knew with one hundred percent certainty that he could help her ...that way.

In a woman's mind —and William feels this way too— there should be no doubt about the worth of what she is giving *and* what she is capable of, *if* the man treats her right. (Assesses to see if Jillian is taking that in)

As for your next thought ...I've never been jealous. Not for a moment. I've been happy for Caitlin, all along, joyously; for how she was growing and what she's become.

If they were together while I was dating someone, I'd never think about him and her. I was involved with who I was with. And if I weren't dating someone at the time and the thought came up, I'd just smile. Once, when I was folding laundry I even laughed out loud, recalling her saying, "I feel it's all brand new. A Midsummer Night's Dream? A Late Twenty's Transformation!"

I told her *not* to give me any details but to savor them for herself. I had known with complete certainty that it was going to be a psychological thing much more than a physical thing, although that was going to be a beautiful thing too. Most of all I wanted him to repair her confidence.

And as far as your next thought is concerned, I was happy and am happy for William! ...Did the few times they were together, maybe ten or twenty, take anything away from me? From me and him? Not at all. And when he and I were together, I never thought about him with her, and I am certain he never did in the reverse. I'd bet on it.

JILLIAN (Pensive) You've said so much. I don't know what to say.

ROBERTA I know. ...But, while you're thinking, Jillian —and this is even more unusual and important— the *guy* you're with has *revealed* all this to his new love.

(Pauses to let her digest) He wants you to know him. To really know him. Both in his unique positive ways and in his ...idiosyncratic ways.

JILLILAN (Smiles at the wording)

ROBERTA Which includes us.

JILLIAN Would you be his unique positive, or his "idiosyncratic," way? (All laugh)

ROBERTA (Smiles) Most guys would have skated over the depth of our relationships and feelings for each other. And left out the physical part entirely! (Holds Jillian's eyes) But that would be a disaster for you and him, eventually. And most guys would have continued without your knowledge *behind* your back, if they could —what I mean is— if I permitted it or if Caitlin did. I'm sure you can believe *that*.

JILLIAN Oh I sure can!

ROBERTA I know him very well. You might say we're kindred spirits. I know how he tunes into people and if that person is a special female, how he thrills to develop her. There were not many in his life —don't go magnifying that in your imagination— but there were some. The best thrill for him is in the development, not in the conquest. ...I credit that as positive. Very. And if not unique, hard to find.

JILLIAN *That,* I know.

ROBERTA William has risked your disapproval, even you bailing out, because he wants you to really know him.

JILLIAN Whew, I knew today would be *interesting.* I appreciate your honesty. ...By the way, I like the way you speak. You sound a lot like William.

CAITLIN And he hasn't given us the slightest nod as to what we should tell you or not tell you. Especially the latter.

JILLIAN I didn't think he would.

CAITLIN Roberta and I are genuinely hoping to develop a friendship with you. ...I have to excuse myself and get dinner ready. (Goes to the kitchen)

ROBERTA What really matters is that he really trusts you.

JILLIAN (Pensive)

ROBERTA Most women wouldn't have been able to meet us. Or they would have done so only to gather ammunition. I think that's because of a basic insecurity, and cultural conditioning. That's my opinion. But the average woman would say I lack self-respect or integrity.

JILLIAN Hardly. (Breath short) This conversation is like nothing I've ever experienced before. ...Except with William.

CAITLIN (From the kitchen) The paella is almost ready. Are the serving utensils out? ...I hope he returns soon.

(Doorbell rings. Quizzical looks all around. Then laughter.)

ROBERTA (To Jillian) I know, I know, I sometimes think he has radar. (All laugh)

WILLIAM (Like Santa Claus with a bag of toys) Here we are! Four different kinds of beer! I think beer goes better with paella than wine. ...Caitlin, that smells *so* good.

ACT II

SCENE 5

Roberta's and Caitlin's apartment, later that evening.

CAITLIN So ...?

ROBERTA What, "So ...?"

CAITLIN (Laughs) Come on! You haven't said anything yet! ...What do you think of her?

ROBERTA I didn't want to influence you in any way. I was waiting for you to bring it up.

CAITLIN Ughh! You're *so* like him! Come on, tell me! I *am* an adult you know, and have an independent mind.

ROBERTA No. You first!

CAITLIN Oooh, *you*! (Both laugh) .... First, she is so open. And honest! For someone to be able to endure what we talked about is extraordinary. ...I like her. I like her a lot! She is sweet and spunky. I can imagine loving her as a sister.

ROBERTA Yep. I know. It's that that he's fallen in love with. Her openness and honesty. That's what opened his trust in her. She's like a kitten, real cute, but that's not the key.

CAITLIN (Pivoting abruptly) Could you do without him? Even occasionally?

ROBERTA I don't know, honestly. I do love our hanging out and our conversations and most of all the simple rapport of our minds. I cherish that the most.

CAITLIN I know. But the other part?

ROBERTA ...I'd hate it ...but yes, I could. I suspect I'd have to. I could.

CAITLIN I would too, but you two have an extra thing. I would miss his company and sharing.

ROBERTA I know. But I want a man of my own, all my own.

ACT II

SCENE 6

William's apartment, one week later.

JILLIAN Aren't you going to ask something about how I think it went?

WILLIAM I don't want to solicit. No. I want you to tell me unasked. And unfiltered.

JILLIAN (To herself aloud) Where to start? Okay, soul level.

First, I have to say, I hate the idea of sharing you, even partially, even sporadically.

I've questioned myself, Why? Why not? If it's very sporadic and it doesn't threaten our relationship, will it be all right? Could it be?

I don't like the idea of you giving to anyone else what you give to me. I'd like to have you exclusively. Permanently exclusively. But I'm learning how you are, essentially, and I also see how they are.

I like them. I didn't want to. They're grounded. And their honesty is astonishing. I thought that one or both would be airheads — "whatever-floats-your-boat" types— whores, really. I was pretty sure I'd walk away with a bad vibe. They're not that way at all. They're balanced. They went out of their way to make me comfortable. I really appreciated that.

And I am getting more of a sense of who you are; how you love.

WILLIAM I knew if you gave them a chance it would go this way.

JILLIAN It wasn't easy, but they were so encouraging and supportive of me with you. No claiming an inside track on you. No hidden putdowns. No envy. I don't understand it. They're genuinely happy for me and you. ...I didn't go in thinking I'd come out with these impressions.

WILLIAM (Smiles) I'm so relieved. I knew it could be like this.

If you were like most women you would have gone in prejudiced and found reasons for your prejudgments, or invented them. Most women would have declared them morally or intellectually defective. And if you weren't as honest and fair-minded as you are, our whole relationship would have crashed long ago. I've been telling you you're different.

JILLIAN They're both smart. Particularly Roberta. And I got a kick out of how Roberta speaks. I see why the two of you get along so easily. She sounds a lot like you.

WILLIAM It's not just smart. It's other things too, like humor and balance. ...Like you, but different.

JILLIAN I know, I was just focusing on that. ...You know, I'd like to see one or both of them again. Without you. Would you mind?

WILLIAM Mind! I'd be delighted! So soon? I'm surprised and delighted. Overwhelmed, actually.

JILLIAN As *you* say, Why waste time? ...Oh, wait a minute. Another thing. Roberta said you are very particular about the women you date, that you are discriminating. Tell me how you screen women. This should be a hoot.

WILLIAM (Smiles) Well, first of all, they have to not be crazy.

JILLIAN (With a Who-doesn't-know-that look) Duhhhh.

WILLIAM (Smiles) No matter how beautiful she is. No matter how much fun it would be to fuck her or whatever, I won't mess with her if she shows signs of the CBG.

JILLIAN The CBG?

WILLIAM The Crazy-Bitch Gene. (Jillian laughs. William smiles.) You know, a Narcissist or Fatal-Attraction type.

JILLIAN I'm glad I escaped those categories. (Both smile) So that makes me special?

WILLIAM You'd be surprised. And you're much more than *not* those things.

ACT II

SCENE 7

William's apartment. A few weeks later. After breakfast.

WILLIAM You look especially nice for a Saturday morning. What's the occasion?

JILLIAN I have a "date."

WILLIAM May I not know a bit more about that? Where are you going and with whom?

JILLIAN We're going to the Frick Museum and then to lunch.

WILLIAM Sounds good. And may I know with whom?

JILLIAN With one of your friends.

WILLIAM Really? Good! Which one?

JILLIAN Does it matter?

WILLIAM Yes. Shouldn't I know? You're very coy this morning.

JILLIAN No, you shouldn't! To be forthright, after lunch, if things go well, we'll head back to my place.

WILLIAM Fine. No mystery there. Why are you making this mysterious?

JILLIAN There, I'm going to make out with her, and kiss her breasts, and suck and lightly bite her nipples, and finger her, and go down on her. And let her reciprocate.

WILLIAM (Dumbfounded)

JILLIAN (Teacher-ish tone) I missed the obligatory lesbian college experience. So I'm going to catch up. The Frick and a fuck.

WILLIAM (Clears his throat) Ah, hmm. This is very interesting. I'd enjoy the comedy more if I knew whether you're satiric or serious.

JILLIAN (Blank face)

WILLIAM You're busting me, right?

JILLIAN (Inscrutable)

WILLIAM You're fucking with my mind, right?

JILLIAN You decide.

WILLLIAM (The echo rings in his mind. His thoughts in rapid fire: she's doing this scene very well; she's confronting the issue on the deepest level; I could find out in a minute; no, I'll let this play out, if there is a "this.")

JILLIAN (Light, breezy voice) See you this evening!

(Uncharacteristically, she leaves the door half-open. A mild breeze from the window pushes it closed with a soft slam.)

ACT II

SCENE 8

Jillian and Roberta. After the museum and a lot of girl-talk and a walk to midtown, they're at a swank restaurant with a reasonable pre-fixe lunch menu.

JILLIAN Now, listen, I've been holding this in since we met. I'm bursting to tell you this!

ROBERTA You look like you're going to burst! What?

JILLIAN I am. You're going to howl!

ROBERTA I'm always up for a good laugh. What?

JILLIAN You won't believe what I pulled on William!

ROBERTA What?

JILLIAN I told him that after the museum, we'd probably go back to my place, (laughs) ...and make out and make love. And I didn't tell him who, which of you, I'd be with!

ROBERTA (Speechless)

JILLIAN I think I did it perfectly. He doesn't know whether I'm serious or busting his balls.

ROBERTA (Trying to roll with what she's just heard) You *are* adorable Jillian, but I don't fancy you that way. Besides, I had the required les moment in college. It didn't get very far. I wasn't really interested, so the experiment failed.

JILLIAN (Smiling, struggling to contain another burst of laughter) No, no, no. That's not the *point*! I *confounded* him! I don't think he's felt like that since he was six years old!

ROBERTA Oh. ...Oh, it's dawning on me. The reason you did it. I'm getting it! ...Beautiful! (Big smile) Good for you! The comedy.

JILLIAN Right! So he'd *feel* all that I'm going through trying to balance his "unique positive" and his "idiosyncratic" ways.

ROBERTA I *love* it! I *knew* there was a deep pool of feisty in you! And William needs that too. Once in a while you *should* off-balance him! It's good for him. (Reaches across the table to embrace her.)

JILLIAN (Smiles in acknowledgement. Welcomes the embrace.)

ACT II

SCENE 9

Two weeks later. Roberta's apartment. Jillian enters.

JILLIAN Hello!

CAITLIN and ROBERTA Hi!

ROBERTA This would have been a delightful surprise if you had just popped over, but since you arranged it, I can't greet you with that line. Nevertheless, it is a delight to see you again.

(Jillian enters. Awkward mood. A few hesitant stabs at small talk.)

ROBERTA I'll get some cools drinks. (Goes to kitchen)

ROBERTA (Returns with iced teas. Senses mood. She and Caitlin exchange glances.)

(Silence)

CAITLIN Say Jillian. It will be all right.

JILLIAN You both have given me a lot to think about. Too much maybe. But since you come in William's wake, or alongside him in a sense, I've had to really think about things.

What do *I* want? Who sets the rules for people? Even, ...is William worth it?

(Jillian scans Roberta and Caitlin) About the last question, I think I know my answer.

But I still have so many questions. How come I don't know any people, women, who talk about these things? How can it work? Are there couples who aren't swingers but do have occasional playmates, and Can some of these also be friends? Can these friendships last for the long haul? Can the primary relationship?

CAITLIN Good questions. We too have had to think about them. All of them. ...I want to be married someday. And to be a Mom.

JILLIAN What are your questions? Besides mine?

CAITLIN Besides yours.... Can I, should I, keep from my husband how absolutely important William has been to me? Should I tell him that someone, named William, —not exactly a boyfriend, and not exactly— ...how could I put it?

Also, who would *believe* it? ...Not exactly a boyfriend; not exactly a therapist although he was that, and an improv coach; definitely my sister's closest confidant and lover for a long time. Would he believe it? And *be okay* with it? Would he *be glad* for my growth?

...I don't *think* so! I'll just have to have that knowledge as my own private history, running in the background. That's my answer.

JILLIAN At least I've been spared *that* problem, ...whether to tell William about "William." (All laugh)

But try as I have to resolve this, I can't. I have a buzz in my head. I didn't expect to like you both. I didn't want to. But I do. And worse

...I respect you. (All laugh) You are sisters, and you've shared him, and do sometimes, or have sometimes, intermittently, or something like that. How do you keep it separate? How come you're not *jealous*? How do you *do* it?

ROBERTA I've tried to answer that. Let me try another perspective. As far as jealousy goes, I knew William could help her. Absolute certainty. Full stop. I wanted the best for Caitlin. Again, full stop.

...No, I'll give you more. She *changed* from whatever they did. Her step was lighter, she smiled more, and her wit was quicker. She challenged me more and I enjoyed it! She grew. She became the confident person you see now.

I should have deprived her of that when I *knew* this would be the outcome? That would have been, *"moral,"* and this, *"immoral*?"

Next ...suppose you had met us at a party, and we weren't sisters. Let's say we were friends, even close friends, and you later learned that we had enjoyed him at one time or another. Would that be better?

JILLIAN I guess so, but this is emotional not logical. I don't know.

ROBERTA Jillian, I am speaking emotionally. William has given me extraordinary experiences. I'm talking about soul experiences. Many times he and I wouldn't even have to say in words what we felt. We read each other. We could just look at each other and have full confirmation of communication. I love him for that. And make sure you take that right, please, I'm talking mentally and emotionally even more than physically. They're connected, but I'm talking *full* person, soul. He gets me. Like no one else has. And I feel honored that he feels that way about me.

Now you are his love object, his focus. I'm not jealous of you. I am very, very happy for you. And for him. I'm so happy he's found someone he loves and wants to be with. It delights me.

And I too want to be married someday. I've also been thinking about how all this will play out.

JILLIAN Would you share this background truth with your husband?

ROBERTA I didn't *need* William sexually-emotionally. But once we connected, I wanted his friendship. But we were —or are, if you'll allow it to continue— dear friends. Nevertheless, to your question, I doubt it. Simply because to reveal our truth and fold William into the mix —historically as a lover— would require a six sigma.

JILLIAN A six *sigma*?

ROBERTA One in a million. That man would have to be one in a million. I think most men are at bottom more insecure sexually. He might get uncomfortable seeing how easily we communicate.

It exaggerates my point, but even a male who is very secure would not tolerate *full* reciprocity with me, hypothetically. You know who I might mean? (All laugh)

JILLIAN Yes, he gave me a short version of your discussion.

CAITLIN And I feel that what I've experienced with him is a very pure thing. I treasure it.

ROBERTA Caitlin and I love William and we've wanted him to find someone really special. And he found you. We're happy for him and for you. If you go forward as a couple that may change things, but I hope it doesn't. Or if it does, I hope it does so only minimally.

It's up to you, ultimately.

JILLIAN (Visibly relieved) I cannot tell you how much you're saying this means to me. But I still don't know. ...You know, interacting with you two is like nothing I've ever experienced. Everything goes so fast, so honest, so deep. It takes my breath away.

ROBERTA Of course! And you have a lot riding on this, Jillian. This is all new territory for us too, I think the only thing we can do is let our hearts guide us.

JILLIAN That sounds right. We'll just have to see. I have to be going now, thanks.

ACT II

SCENE 10

William's apartment, a week later. William and Jillian.

WILLIAM It's been quite a while. I'll solicit.

JILLIAN What?

WILLIAM How did it go? Your "date." Your mystery date three weeks ago?

JILLIAN Oh, that. Great. We had a lovely time.

WILLIAM More than that, please. You know what I'm really asking.

JILLIAN (Momentarily undecided about which way to play it, then....) It went very well. Great. She has a nice body and she's quite *responsive.* And we talked and fantasized during it. Like you and I do sometimes.

WILLIAM (Blinks, slight frown) You're *busting* me again. Right?

JILLIAN You'll never know.

WILLIAM I could find out in a minute.

JILLIAN I don't think so.

WILLIAM (Long pause. His pulse quickening.) Hon, I get it. It's really hard. Even with the best intentions, it is hard.

JILLIAN *Good!* Now you know, "...from your body up to your mind!"

ACT II

SCENE 11

Walking through Prospect Park. Jillian and Caitlin.

JILLIAN I love this park.

CAITLIN It's my first time here. I think it's more beautiful than Central Park.

JILLIAN Well, Olmstead designed it later than Central Park. There are no transverses to think about and it feels more spacious. No tall buildings hemming the borders. ...A great place to almost forget about civilization.

CAITLIN Roberta told me about what you pulled on William! That was so funny. I couldn't stop laughing.

JILLIAN It was such a hoot!

CAITLIN Jillian, I have to risk something. I don't want to spoil the mood, or get too heavy, but I have to tell you something. It would linger under the surface and I don't want that. If I don't open this up I will feel unclean.

JILLIAN Oh boy, this is gonna be a *doozie*! I can feel it.

CAITLIN I gave William what I considered to be a "promissory note" of thanks. I was so grateful for his integrating my mind and body, his gift to me, that I told him ...that even if I were married ...I would gladly blow him any time he wished. (Urgently) Please hear me out. Please don't say anything yet!

JILLIAN (Brow furrowed) I'm listening.

CAITLIN Jillian ...I know this sounds very provocative, but understand that the gift he gave me was so powerful and so respectfully given, that I gave him that promise out of elation. I knew it was naughty, but I also knew the chances of the promise coming to fruition were close to zero anyway. I've thought a lot about it. I've decided to retract my "promissory note." I'm healed. It's the right thing to do for you and me, and for you and him. I know that I didn't have to confess this to you, and I didn't want to hurt you, but I want to be completely honest. You are such a beautiful person. I want your friendship and I don't want anything in the way of that. Nothing hidden.

I'm growing to love you. Actually, I admire you.

JILLIAN (Long pause) Thank you. (Tears in her eyes) For all that.

(Jillian and Caitlin stop walking, look at each other, and hug.)

ACT II

SCENE 12

William and Jillian, walking through Washington Square Park.

JILLIAN Guess what Caitlin and I talked about on our lovely walk in Prospect Park? Clear out of the blue, Caitlin made a confession to me. No, that's not accurate. No guilt. She confided her "promissory note."

WILLIAM Uh hmm.

JILLIAN She retracted it.

WILLIAM I know. She called me.

...You may find this surprising, Jill, but I'm happy for her. And for you.

JILLIAN (Question written on her brow)

WILLIAM For her, because it had to come sometime. And, I feel she has given me a bouquet of flowers. Her lasting appreciation. I love that. ...It doesn't have to be the other thing.

And I'm happy for you, because it takes a worry off your plate —a needless worry in my view— but I understand. I know what you worry about ...that I might desire her or anyone more than you, but that would not happen. And I know that if she didn't see in you what I see, she mightn't have retracted her Thank You note. She'd have stretched out her time with me, like a patient who can't let go of their psychotherapy even though they're fully fledged.

JILLIAN (Softly) I wish you had retracted it first.

WILLIAM Why? It's actually better that Caitlin came to this decision herself, first, alone. This way she doesn't feel interrupted, that she's not quite one hundred percent healed. She determined her own growth state. It's better. Really.

JILLIAN My past experiences were so different, (shakes her head in anger), I *never* would have given anything *close* to a promissory note to *any* of them. Not close!

I'm coming to appreciate all that you've given Caitlin. Like what you've given me. I get it now. (Voice cracks) And that makes me realize even more what I never got.

WILLIAM (Holds her) What you never got, until *me*. (Kisses her tears, then her cheeks and mouth)

JILLIAN Yes. What you give me. (Smiles, recovers herself) But don't you be getting a big head now.

ACT II

SCENE 13

William and Jillian at Roberta's door.

ROBERTA Hi guys!

WILLIAM and JILLIAN Hello.

ROBERTA (Gestures Come in, Hugs both)

WILLIAM Listen, I know you're not *savages* (all laugh) but I'm very hungry. Suppose I go get some Chinese and some beer?

ROBERTA (Shares a look with Jillian and a smile) Okay.

JILLIAN Yes. Go "dash." We women need to talk.

WILLIAM Good, go ahead. (Exits)

JILLIAN I need you to talk with me truly like sisters. You both have had such different experiences than me.

CAITLIN Not so very different, mine, Jillian, before William.

JILLIAN Okay, I hear you. (Audible outbreath) Just rehearsing this in my mind makes me feel funny, embarrassed, but I have to blurt this out. I always thought that... no, that's not right.... In my high school all the girls who were popular, or most of the desirable ones were doing it, or at least I heard them making jokes about doing it.

I got to think,... no, ...I believed, that it was what all those girls did, especially if they had a boyfriend and wanted to please him.

CAITLIN I know what you are stumbling to say. Please just say it. I'll answer you honestly.

(Both Roberta and Caitlin wait for Jillian to be one step more specific.)

JILLIAN Besides, you couldn't get pregnant from doing it.

CAITLIN Uh hmm.

JILLIAN What are your attitudes about doing it? (Blushing)

ROBERTA (After a brief pause in which she glances at Caitlin and returns her eyes to Jillian.) In a nutshell, it shouldn't be done transactionally. You know what I mean?

JILLIAN (Mortified; trying not to show it.)

ROBERTA (To make sure she's not misunderstood.) This, for a relationship. She has to be doing it for the right reasons.

JILLIAN (Using the term to help herself recover.) The "right" reasons?

ROBERTA Actually, what the wrong reasons are, is the better question. It shouldn't be to win him over or to keep him dating her, or because you can't get pregnant from doing it.

(Emotion again crosses Jillian's face, she suppresses it.)

The right reason? It must be because she appreciates what he gives to her, what he does for her, that she wants to give back to him and she chooses that way. Because he's really into you, and your unconflicted desire about wanting to do it, for yourself and for him.

Of course, there is another possibility, if they recently met and she just wants to, or wants to prove she's cool, or equal to men, or that she has no hang-ups. But why the need to prove? Anyway, in that case, it'll probably be a short-term thing. 'Just gave him a blow job. Ha, ha. No big whoops.'

JILLIAN Is that one out of ten?

ROBERTA (Laughs) No, maybe three or four today. ...It shouldn't be trivialized. There is something extra special about that act, I feel.

JILLIAN I wish I'd had a friend who I could've talked with about all this. My mother's advice was sex after marriage. That was it. She gave me a book to read about puberty. I wasn't even prepared for my period, it came as a shock to me. I had to figure it out on my own.

ROBERTA and CAITLIN (Nod)

JILLIAN (Pondering) I couldn't have this conversation with *any* of my friends. There was always such a cloud of mystery about sexual things. They'd joke about it, but never reveal how they feel about any particular act. I don't know any women who talk like we're talking.

ROBERTA Well maybe they *should*. Aren't we learning from each other? We speak honestly and without ulterior motives. You're learning, from us, and I'm learning from you.

JILLIAN You are?

ROBERTA I have more reason to respect you because I see your growth and I know you more intimately. I feel your fundamental decency, and honesty.

Listen, William explained a concept from his field, "the pathology of normalcy." Basically, conformity. That's what you and your reference group and most folks did. Sought to conform. The sexual fallout of that is girls ignoring their feelings and going along with cultural expectations. Just look at what's on TV.

JILLIAN You're right. I ignored and pretended, and made normal what I knew in my heart was not right. I thought I had to.

CAITLIN I am right there with you, Jillian. I got caught up in it too. I wasn't honest with myself about some guys who I idealized. I had unrealistic hopes and tried to make relationships work that were not proving out.

Jillian, here's my soul.... I cannot be more honest with you. You know that William connected my mind and body. But more than that, he connected my mind, *heart*, and body. What I would allow now, would do or not do, is an integrated circuit, Me. I was disconnected before. I might never have fully integrated or it might have taken years, if Roberta hadn't "shared" him with me. At bottom, it had to do with my feelings of self-worth.

JILLIAN (Nods)

(Lost in thought: That's right, but it can't be right. You're sisters. And William was *her* lover. Or is sometimes, but less often now. But they still love each other. And I do love Caitlin. And I respect Roberta so much. I'm starting to love her too though her mind intimidates me at times. She thinks so acutely, so fast, and puts things so well. Right down to essence. But I don't want her to have had William. That's crazy, all that was before he and I ever met. I don't want her to have William. But what's wrong with that, occasionally? I see them interacting. They're beautiful friends, I really believe she's not a rival. Caitlin had him "occasionally," not more, and they're not rivals. That didn't harm anything. It helped Caitlin. But they're sisters. It's incest. No, it's not. Then what is it? Why do I think it's wrong? 'Judge from the results.' It's right. And they both agree and are at peace with it. Happy about it. Who's to say it's wrong? Maybe in some circumstances it's okay. Maybe in this circumstance it's good. I don't know. Oh, this is exhausting!)

ROBERTA (Reading her) Let's take a break. How about a gin and tonic? Would you like one?

JILLIAN I'd love it, thanks. (Roberta goes to kitchen)

CAITLIN I hear it all the time, crass jokes about sexual acts, especially this one, from some men, and nowadays some women. 'If all of us make cracks about it, it can't be a big deal.' 'It's just a thing, no big deal.' But that's transparently defensive, even if they don't know it.

JILLIAN Yeah, that sounds like some of the girls I went to school with, in high school and college.

(Roberta returns with drinks)

JILLIAN This is good! What gin is it?

ROBERTA Tanqueray.

CAITLIN ...Jillian, William has had a good effect on you! Keep letting him grow you and you will grow him in turn.

ROBERTA Yes, and I see your effect on him. He's yours Jillian. You know, we're all trying to balance a complicated story, even beyond him. We're cultural pioneers.

JILLIAN Grow him, that's hard to believe!

ROBERTA Not really. Trust me. You will, believe it now or not.

JILLIAN (Silent. Letting this sink in.) I'd like more ice for my drink. And for my mind. (All laugh) Please bring me a bucket of mind-ice.

CAITLIN Sure, I'll get it.

(Doorbell rings)

ROBERTA Great timing. (Opens the door. William returns with Chinese takeout and beers. Roberta smiling, glances at Jillian.) What do you have ...*radar*? (The three women laugh)

ACT II

SCENE 14

Roberta and Caitlin at home.

CAITLIN Why do you think they haven't called in a while?

ROBERTA I don't know.

CAITLIN Do you think they're fighting?

ROBERTA They have a lot to figure out.

CAITLIN Do you think Jillian will be able to balance out all of this? *You* could do it, but compared to every other woman I've ever met you're more ...*evolved.* I might be able do it now if I had to, but that would be based on your model and only because I've benefited so greatly from him. But I wouldn't want to. I'd be jealous and I don't know any men who would be worthy of that trust.

ROBERTA (Laughs) Right.

CAITLIN But I wouldn't want to. Nor would I want to subject my husband to that test in the reverse.

ROBERTA (Challenging, slightly naughty tone) But you know, sometimes these things come unbidden.

CAITLIN (Goes over and hugs her) I just love you. You're so wicked.

ROBERTA (Hugs back and smiles) It's not as if I would never have to wrestle with letting him have another "playmate" occasionally, if we had married. *But*, if he absolutely *never* gave me reason to suspect that I was slipping into second place, in *any* way, then I could accept it and even in a funny way enjoy it.

CAITLIN How's *that*?!

ROBERTA I might sometimes ask him to share details with me. To know *his* inner experience: the sequence, her resistance if any, the overcoming of her resistance. *That* would be the most interesting!

And to take it away from her! To assert *my* centrality with him through *our* love-making. I could delight in his delight, while powerfully re-bonding him to me through my gifts to him, and re-confirming *our* love by sharing his experience and folding it into our own.

CAITLIN (Smiles, shakes head) "Six sigma?" *You're* six sigma!

ROBERTA (Smiles) I take that as a complement.

CAITLIN. I mean it that way! ...Maybe there are other women who could do that and enrich their relationship, but I don't know of any. (Smiles) Maybe they should make a movie of it.

ROBERTA (Smiles back. No words.)

ACT III

(The Regression)

SCENE 1

William at Jillian's apartment, Friday night, two weeks later.

WILLIAM What?

JILLIAN You know. Or should know.

WILLIAM What? Please, tell me.

JILLIAN That *stupid* play or screenplay you're writing, whatever it is!

WILLIAM The play?

JILLIAN That's right! It's stupid.

WILLIAM What's wrong with it?

JILLIAN Everything!

WILLIAM Say, please....

JILLIAN Is that all you think about, fucking and oral sex with the two of them? *I'll* write a play and *my* play will be about *love*. I will. I'll start *tomorrow*.

WILLIAM (Confused, quiet)

JILLIAN (Insecurity gripping her) And she should give you that promise into the future!

WILLIAM Hold on!

JILLIAN No you hold on! How do you expect me to like them or love them and let them into our future with so much of the past being present!

WILLIAM Wait. In the—

JILLIAN No, you wait. I will not be with someone who expects me to blow him when we go out. I won't have it! I'm sick of it! I've had enough of that in my past.

WILLIAM Jillie, honey,

JILLIAN Don't "honey" me....

WILLIAM In the first place, I have proved over and over with you that I don't expect that! I have even refused to let you, time and time again. Isn't that so?

JILLIAN Yes. But it feels like that now. She will blow you on demand.

WILLIAM What 'demand,' Jill, honey? There is no 'demand.' I'm not like that. Just the opposite! She gave me that promise out of exuberance! Sheer exuberance. To let me know that she will always appreciate what I did for her.

JILLIAN But it's there for the taking. She retracted it, but I'm sure you could get her to reinstate it with one meeting.

WILLIAM It's there, or was there, but I didn't dream it up. I even refused you early on! I told you, Not until I think you're ready! *I* insisted. How many guys do you think would do *that*? Pass that up? A *guy* told you "No!" *This* guy told you No. *Me*. Remember?

JILLIAN (Silent)

WILLIAM I am differently composed, damn it. And I think my ingredients are pretty well-balanced. An unusual blend, Yes. So much so that I've never run across anybody like me, except one, in female form. And, No, I don't think so. Caitlin told you that because she's grown and because she respects you. She wouldn't reinstate it just upon a phone call or meeting.

JILLIAN (Absorbing, but trying to recover her feisty self.) *You* can be pretty persuasive.

WILLIAM (Angrily) Now stop it! (Catches himself. Immediately changes register completely. No hint of irony.) Yes, ...you're right. I'll explain. Caitlin wants to be faithful when she's married so she will fuck only her husband. But a blow job on the side, for me, doesn't count. It's just a side gig. And besides, I bought a bicycle bell.

JILLIAN (Brow furrowed. Looks like, Where the hell is this going?) William, what the heck are you talking about?

WILLIAM (Teacher-ish voice) We've arranged it, that when I call for one, I won't *say* anything. Nothing, just ring the bell. That way she won't have to lie to her husband outright. Only half-lie. She'll just tell him, "It's that kid again, the one who doesn't say anything and just rings a bell. He or she must be a little off."

JILLIAN (Caught in a cross-current of emotions: anger at the imagery's possibility, anger at him using this ridiculous imagery which she doesn't really believe, feels mocked, and self-humiliated knowing that she had instigated his satire.)

WILLIAM (Releasing her from the satire) *Please*! She's not a call girl! And I wouldn't just call her for a blow job. Do you not know me? How I *am*? Please get yourself together! This whole conversation is jinking off on a tangent. (Long pause)

JILLIAN (Ignoring, unable to let go of the image.) Okay, But how do you expect me to deal with it? Here you have the Great Male Fantasy: *three* women loving you to pieces, not just two! Three! Willing to fuck you and suck you, every time you meet! Even eager to. You are too much! You're asking too much of me. Go find another woman who's able and willing to deal with it!

WILLIAM Please calm down. My relationship with them has already changed. And that's because of our relationship. I want you. They predated our relationship.

JILLIAN I know that. It doesn't matter. What if they didn't *pre*date? Suppose you had met *after* us?

WILLIAM Would you wish to deprive me of a beautiful friendship? Even *after*?

Mindsharing at the level that you know about, that you have witnessed and have experienced directly yourself, and have benefited from? Would you wish me *not* to have it? So what if it happened *after*? Should I *not* have it? You would wish me not to?

And would it have been better for *you* to have never known her, and them?

JILLIAN ...No. Yes. Maybe. ...The physical side frightens me.

WILLIAM Why? I govern myself. You know *why* I've been with Caitlin, and you've seen how I *am* with her. Is there something wrong that I'm not acknowledging?

And, you know how my relationship with Roberta has evolved.

...Jill, I'm willing to rethink anything for you, but I'm not following your reasoning. We, you and I, have so much already and have so much promise.

JILLIAN I don't want to lose you. I get scared, William. You've made everything so wonderful.

WILLIAM Yes ...What are you saying?

JILLIAN I'm saying that I don't want to feel that I'm ...*competing*! With her. Or her. Or both of them. ...Or anyone. Ever! (Jillian's face turns to sad/vulnerable. William embraces her. She relaxes a little, allows the embrace to calm her, then returns the embrace.)

WILLIAM Jillian, I'll think over what you wish me to rethink. I'm not resisting here, but answer this, Have you ever had any doubts caused by me, at all? Have I given you the slightest indication, ever, in all of our intimacies, that I was not with you totally? Or that I ever compared you?

JILLIAN No. But I am still upset. I try, but I can't completely reconcile all this.

WILLIAM What do you want me to rethink?

JILLIAN I don't want you to ever think of them, either of them, especially Roberta, and find me deficient in any way.

WILLIAM Jillian, you've explored and let me explore, and let me teach you your sexuality far more than anyone you've ever been with. I cherish that. Now, you're spinning yourself into confusion. I have never thought of Roberta, *ever*, when I've been with you.

JILLIAN (No answer)

WILLIAM Not once. Nor Caitlin either. I am not like that. I'm totally with the woman I'm with. How do you think I read you so well?

And "deficient?" I wouldn't be with you if I thought that. ...Come on!

JILLIAN (Long silence) Aren't I enough?

WILLIAM (Resignedly) I suppose that's the inevitable question. But it is not the right question, for me. A question has to be species-specific: you can't test a fish by seeing how it flies. I'm sorry, Jill, but when I love, I love intensely and faithfully —let me *finish*— but how I am....

I'm stumped how be honest and put this right....

Listen, regarding this issue, I feel like I'm running down a platform hoping to leap onto a departing train, and I have to run fast to maybe catch the caboose railing. If I do, I can enjoy the ride through life. If I don't, then life, even with someone I truly and deeply love, will feel partially like a cage.

JILLIAN I wouldn't want to cage you, but you want your cake and to eat it too.

WILLIAM Yes, but. My "cake" menu is a distinctly limited one. I have many screens. The great majority of cakes are rejected.

JILLIAN But still, it's not fair.

WILLIAM Fair. ...You want the same freedom?

JILLIAN No. I want the security of having no rivals!

WILLIAM I'm telling you that you do, and you will.

JILLIAN Please, William, fill in the missing pieces!

WILLIAM You do have that security, and you will have no rivals.

JILLIAN You can't know that. I love that you say that, but you can't know that.

WILLIAM There's a lot about life we can't know, like what's coming around the corner, but I know this as well as I can know anything. I'm an extremely reflective person as you know, and I know myself fairly well. I'm aware of the elements that combine to make me who I am. I'm telling you, from the deepest core of my truth-center and to the extent that anyone can predict their future feelings, that I love you and will continue to, faithfully. This is me and this is how I am.

JILLIAN (Exhausted) I wish you came differently combined.

(Pause. Mood lightening.) But you don't. Part of me wants to change you but I am attracted to you as you are. You've been so open and honest with me, it softens my heart. I do believe we can be happy.

(Mild resignation, with mild self-mockery) I want you more than anyone I've ever been with. I'd rather suffer occasional uncertainty with you, than live without you.

WILLIAM Thank you for even trying that on. I will try to eliminate every uncertainty, but any that remain are yours. ...We all have private moments of doubt.

JILLIAN You just said you have no doubt about your love and your continuing love for me.

WILLIAM I wasn't referring to that. I meant that everyone has moments of doubt, like, Am I right? and, Can I be totally sure? I don't bullshit myself into thinking that I'm clairvoyant.

JILLIAN Oh.

WILLIAM Everyone has private doubts. Me included. I use my doubts to test myself. Constantly. They're my acid test to refine my beliefs.

JILLIAN So, how do we reconcile this? ...All right, I'll take the lead. You told me why you fell in love with me. I fell in love with you because of all that you gave me and your humor, and your mind. Vastly more than anyone else had given me. More than all combined. And you want my feelings and demand my mind.

WILLIAM Right. That's right!

JILLIAN Not just sex "transactionally." (Smiles to herself)

WILLIAM (Sees it, smiles)

JILLIAN (Annoyed and pleased) Why are you smiling? You look like a possum!

WILLIAM You know.

JILLIAN No I don't.

WILLIAM (Teasingly) Yes you do.... (Rubbing it in) I know.

JILLIAN You know what?

WILLIAM (Breaking the tease) Where you got that word from.

(Jillian looks annoyed at first but then smiles. Both smile. No words. Long pause.)

JILLIAN What things do I have to rethink?

WILLIAM What you said before that you are "sick of" and that you're sorry for it now. *Why* is that?

JILLIAN (No answer)

WILLIAM Why are you sorry for that now?

JILLIAN (No answer)

WILLIAM You're sorry because *how* I love you has given you perspective! You understand things about yourself now because of my love and how I give it to you, and how I want you to feel it. My whole body smiles seeing you feel the love I feel for you.

JILLIAN (Beaming) And my whole body smiles back. It's true, none of them ever immersed themselves in me. Especially my first one. It was expected that I had to leap into sex without even thinking about what I wanted and was ready for. And with no 'grooming,' no loving build up.

WILLIAM That's right. If you wanted to be his girlfriend, right from the start. But worse, *you* then internalized it, and still worse, *you* made it *habit*! That's what hurts me the most! He cracked the whip and you capitulated. Without requiring that *you* be properly given to!

Why you capitulated is what you have to rethink! And that will also involve thinking about your parents and what they neglected to give you. Your whole past locked you in. Until now.

JILLIAN (Silent)

WILLIAM I don't consent to the conditioning our culture imposes on me, and you. We can work things out for ourselves.

You know, there's a fascinating and terrifying neurological condition called Locked-In Syndrome. Look it up later if you wish. Sometimes I view society as both suffering from and inflicting on us a form of Locked-In Syndrome.

(Pause) Back to you. Until you get to the bottom of why you expected to do you know what, you won't be free to experience me fully and clearly. You didn't have to do that.

JILLIAN (Unable to meet his eyes)

WILLIAM You gave, in hope of a relationship, based on nothing! Fantasy. Illusion.

JILLIAN (Still unable to meet his eyes)

WILLIAM Never! Not unless they *deserved* it and *you* wanted to. Both! Above all, that they *deserved* it! ...If not, then *never!* As in, not ever. You get it? Not with him, them, or me. *Not even with me.*

JILLIAN (Tears silently at his last words)

WILLIAM (Goes to her and holds her) You're glad for me, I know you love me, madly, but sometimes —like now— your past re-takes you. You conflate them with me. Don't do that. Please.

And even if once in a great while, with another woman, ...you needn't worry. And I'll *prove* that claim right now!

You are living proof! I knew you would come away feeling differently if you met Roberta and Caitlin. You originally thought they must be whores. You had other negative prejudgments that also turned out to be wrong. You've seen the results from three angles, yours and theirs. And if you include me in the picture, four.

Next; I know that I'll prove out for the long haul. My love for you won't get knocked off course or fade. If anything, it will grow stronger because of what you occasionally gift me. You'll have to trust me on that. Verify, of course, but give me a *chance* to prove out.

Our culture "locks in" that what I'm asking for is preposterous and wrong, but it's not —for some people. Maybe what the culture dictates is all right for some people, but not for others. And I am *not* saying that I'm so fucking wonderful, but I am differently combined. I'm not just a dick who wants to score with any nice-looking thing in a skirt. I've told you, and I think Roberta has told you, and Caitlin has told you, how I love, and what the best thrill is for me.

Proof three? I didn't want you just for your body. You'd have allowed me or given it —you offered it— but I insisted that we get our minds synchronized. How's *that* for proof!

I'm steady with you. That's how I'll be with you. Have been, am, and will be.

JILLIAN You're rocking my world. You know that. I have to overthrow everything I've taken for granted.

WILLIAM Not everything, but a lot.

There's more and it's important. You have further proof from Caitlin's transformation. I loved helping her re-set her "do" "and allow" switches, and to correct her wrongly set "stop-self" switch. She needed to self-set emotional benchmarks before beginning certain intimacies. Basically, to trust herself, that it was right for her to have those benchmarks.

She respected me, courtesy of Roberta, and liked me. She provisionally trusted that I would take her where she wanted to go. Still, the parameters were way out at the start. But things quickly became good, not weird. We improvised in "live" time, meaning, based on her real feelings. We role-played. I slowed her down. I made her pay attention to her own sensations and, if there were associations that conflicted her, to talk about them and even cry them through. I made her say out loud what she was going through. She resisted at first. Then, she wept. A number of times. This freed her to register her real desires. She began to have fantasies for the first time. I made her say them. She was in the moment. She stopped jumping to end results, either for the other party or herself.

I had the privilege —yes, Jillian, the privilege— of *teaching* her that, and *that* integrated her mind and personality even more than body parts or actions.

Transforming her was a privilege and an honor.

JILLIAN (Mixture of facial expressions)

WILLIAM Jillian, please, I haven't wanted to capture Caitlin, to "have" her permanently, on the side.

And you have to know that Caitlin worked on herself during her …journey. To keep herself from falling in love with me didn't just *happen.* She worked on herself all along. Yes she loves me, and Yes she feels grateful, but she never let herself get into a "must have" need state.

…It was a conscious wrestling match: "The Frontal Lobes versus Oxytocin," was how she put it.

And equally, she cherishes Roberta. She loves her even more because she knows that what Roberta gave her is so outside of society's norms; so "off-the-charts." They both know how society would judge them. despise them. ridicule them. They know. They wouldn't share it with anybody, but they've shared it with you, their *inner* experiences. And I've shared it with you too, willingly. My soul. How beautiful is that?

People wouldn't believe it if they ever discovered it —what you and I are thrashing out— and they would condemn me. I know.

No matter Caitlin's transformation, most of society would not think it beautiful. Her vouching would be swept aside. They'd condemn all of us. And doubly so if we were married, me and you. You know how most of society would judge me. ...Am I that?

When you get scared Jillian, you frighten yourself by imagining that I couldn't possibly sustain my love for you. You're still not convinced, down to your soul, how much you are worth. You are much more desirable than you've ever let yourself think.

If clown number one had appreciated you, your self-confidence would not have been crimped. It would have grown. It should have. He abused you. He hardly gave while he let you give. It disgusts me.

(Not wanting to add, but forcing himself to say it.) And you are responsible too. He had no *right* to you! You should have felt that! You didn't fight him off when he soft-raped you. What he forced you to do.

Also, you disparaged yourself. Before and throughout that relationship, you compared yourself to his previous. So you had better comply —even if you had qualms— and make the best of it.

JILLIAN (Tearing up. Looks away.)

WILLIAM (goes to her, embraces her and gently lifts up her face.) I do *not* compare you, and I *will* not compare you. I love you very deeply, and my consistency will be sealed in our flesh, minds and hearts. Please don't worry. I will prove out. Give us a chance.

JILLIAN (Renewed tearing, but recovering her voice.) I know you love me, I feel it in everything you do.

WILLIAM Hon, we're exhausted. Let's go for a ride. Pack a little bag, right now. Let's just shower and go for a long ride and find a place for the weekend.

JILLIAN (Recovering) Good idea. I'd love a car ride!

ACT III

SCENE 2

Driving on the Palisades Interstate Parkway heading towards a New York State Park. In William's car. Both are taking in the combined haptic joy of that road and the beautiful vistas.

(Jillian releases her seatback a few notches. She knows that her miniskirt will slide up if she lets it and she lets it. It falls back. The lip of her skirt is all the way up. She may even have encouraged it a trifle with her wrist as she slid into the lowered backrest. William is not sure. He sees her legs entirely and sees the white whisper of her panties. He is very delighted and very excited.

Jillian relaxes more hoping that he will touch her. She wants him to touch her. William wants to of course, and Jillian knows this, and also knows that he is purposely not seizing the opportunity, like most guys would. This pleases her, which William wants, and it makes it "worse" for her, because she does more and more urgently want to come from his touch. He knows what she wants. He also wants to prolong his own erotic torture.

He knows that the view is a gift to him —her legs, the whisper of her panties and what is shielded underneath by only a few molecules of cotton or silk— and he knows that her freedom to do this is another gift to him, a display of her jubilant new self-confidence. His heart and mind are thumping.

William debates; Wait a moment, or not? Jillian can take it no longer. She reaches with her left hand for his right hand and cups it on herself. He presses a little, moves his fingertips a little, and then presses hard. Eyes closed, she lets herself release. Then she presses his hand more insistently against her, for comfort and for afterglow. No other guy ever even thought about afterglow. She loves giving him the pleasure of feeling all her internal changes which she knows he loves.

Jillian is pleased with her freedom to express her sexual desires without embarrassment.

William checks the road to see if an exit is coming up soon. No. He reaches across and slips his hand into her panties to feel her directly. Without looking she feels the delight on his face and smiles to herself. She sighs and relaxes more, comforted by his hand on her. She keeps her eyes closed, knowing that he will drive to their destination and not insist on, or even hint at stopping somewhere, so he can get his. Not even the thought of having to repay him. No repayment, no prepayment. Just in-the-moment love. She can simply float. A new psychological landscape. She drifts off into a nap, with his finger and hand on her.)

ACT III
SCENE 3

Dusk the following evening. Jillian and William at a secluded lake, on a large tatami mat in a shady spot under a tree.

JILLIAN What a lovely day, from start to finish. Thank you. (Smiles)

WILLIAM Your welcome. I enjoyed it too. Thoroughly. And thank you too. ...But you're mistaken in one thing.

JILLIAN What's that?

WILLIAM It's not "finished."

(He rolls over and takes her in his arms. Kisses her, and she kisses him back. They make out like that, unhurriedly. Both gradually expand their caressing. He listens to her breath changes, pulls back and smiles. They re-caress and make out some more and he pleasures her breasts, outside first and then inside.)

JILLIAN (Gasps and chuckles) You always make the girls feel so good! (She presses and plays with his front bulge.)

WILLIAM (With his hand in her bikini bottom) Take this off.

(Jillian is momentarily shocked and uncertain, but then re-assures herself that no one is around and that she can rely on him to sacrifice a bit of his pleasure so that she can fully release herself. William would not let anyone see her exposed. She does.

Both continue making out, with passion rising. He presses her legs apart a bit, caresses and fondles her upper inner thighs, cups her cunt, caressing her labia. She opens her legs more and begins responding with her hips. He feels her moist now and circleplays her clitoris, then fingers her, following her rhythm at first, then leading her. Like waves at high tide pounding on the beach she comes, and gasps, and thinks, 'Every time so different.')

WILLIAM (Smiles and whispers) No one should have access to this without kissing you. A lot.

JILLIAN Shush! I know! (Breathlessly) Kiss me! Keep kissing me.

WILLIAM (Laughs)

JILLIAN Uh. (Pause) Uh. (Slightly longer pause) Uh! (Long pause) Oh!

(Jillian very quiet. William cupping her, to let the heat of his whole hand soothe her and to keep the afterglow glowing. Soon after, Jillian draws breath to talk.)

WILLIAM (Prevents her from saying anything by whispering first) And you thought you were defective! (Big smile)

JILLIAN (Goes to say something)

WILLIAM (Interrupts again. Looks at her with total confidence, his eyes commanding like Bela Lugosi's in Dracula.) You have another one up there.

(Jillian looks at him with an astonished, 'You can't know that' look. William starts to kiss her again. They play. She is still wet. He enters her again with his finger. She surrenders.)

JILLIAN Ohhh! Unbelievable! (After recovery) I've never come like this before. In colors!

...You know, I could get addicted to this. (Hugs him tightly) Umm, It's good to be your love-bug. (Kisses him again)

WILLIAM (Smiles. Soul-satisfied. No words.)

ACT III

SCENE 4

Jillian's apartment, midweek, following the getaway.

JILLIAN I'm sorry for my episode the other week. I realize how all over the place I was.

WILLIAM You were scared. ...Thanks for the apology. Apologies always help.

JILLIAN You're welcome. Yes, they do always help.

WILLIAM Yup. For a relationship to last, they're vital. ...I'd put apologies equal to great sex.

JILLIAN (Laughs) You, and sex!

WILLIAM It's never far away from me. It's my shadow. ...Maybe when I'm eighty you won't have to deal with it. (Smiles)

JILLIAN (Obvious irony) Well that's optimistic! At least there's an end date.

WILLIAM (Fake frown, then smiles) There's another, even more "optimistic" benefit in store for you!

JILLIAN What's that?

WILLIAM I'll keep you wide-awake sexually till then.

JILLIAN (Smiles, preparing a repartee....)

WILLIAM You'll be the most sexually alive woman in your age range. Long into menopause and beyond. Long after most womens' libidos are a faded or hibernating memory. (Smiles)

I'll keep you vibrant. (Smiles) Without a vibrator. (Smiles wider) Or with, if you'd like. (Jill returns his wordplay with a smile)

Actually —assuming the woman isn't expressing the C-B Gene— I think that defunct sex between a couple is more often the man's fault. Many guys' think, 'Just fuck me, or suck me and everything'll be fine.' They don't think, 'Can I help the situation?' They don't consider or don't remember that their woman needs an emotional connection. Then women turn off or some have affairs.

I've even told some of my guy patients, '...You want to get into her panties? ...Talk with her!' They always laugh. They think I'm half-joking or they laugh because I used ordinary language.

Half of my gender is out to lunch, asleep at the wheel. And half of your gender has been giving away the farm.

JILLIAN You know, William, my fear comes from the fact that I always want to be your primary trust object, sex object, and love object. I don't want anyone taking you away from me or having an inside track on you that I don't have.

WILLIAM Good. I'm glad you want that. You are that. Be assured that you are all that, trust, sex and love object. Just keep trusting me and loving me. You are central.

I don't want you to ever feel that anyone else has the inside track on me. I'll give you all my "secrets." Willingly. (Smiles) I'll give you something right now if you wish. Where would you like me to begin? What do you want to know?

JILLIAN Everything. From the beginning, if you think that makes sense.

WILLIAM It doesn't, Jillian. There's too much and it will overwhelm you. I'll give you a horse dovery and we'll see how you react to that.

JILLIAN (Deep frown) What the heck is a "horse dovery!?"

WILLIAM I'm playing, hon. (Smiling) An *hors d'oeuvres.*

JILLIAN (Frown-snickers) Oh.

WILLIAM A weak joke, I know. I'm stalling. I'm deciding where to start. What and how much to start with. Any of my childhood's "main courses" would choke a person. It can't be done in one sitting, it's too much.

JILLIAN (Body tenses. Surprised at William's unusual register.)

WILLIAM (Musing aloud) Okay, ...the orchestra warms up. (Gestures like a conductor up-down-stroking) Good, I see that you're sitting.

...I remember being nine and making an appeal to god. Yes. I was innocent and had been brainwashed to believe there was a such a thing. I was on the northwest corner of Foster and East 17th, in Brooklyn —I remember these things precisely, you'll see as you get to know me more— and I tried to make a deal with him.

'Thirty-six. Please. Let me live to be thirty-six. I'll get out of here as soon as I'm eighteen and all I ask is to let me have *half* of my life away from them. Thirty-six, ...it doesn't have to be more.'

JILLIAN (Stunned!)

WILLIAM Here's another one. Let me set this up right.

...I grew up in a War Zone, Jill. A domestic war zone. Behind the door of an ordinary middle, middle-class apartment, my mother and father fought, I'd say, two, three or four days a week. And often their fights were marathon. They'd last for hours. I'm not kidding.

And separately, me and my father were always at war. The two wars intersected, and she was allied with him sort of, but the wars were mostly separate. Mine with him was sometimes hot, sometimes cold, but after age ten I could not stand to be in the same room as him.

JILLIAN (Shocked, appalled and saddened by what she is hearing.)

WILLIAM Jill, there's a book with the title, "Preparation For A Descent Into Hell." That would be an apt title for my childhood. I know that many people have had it worse, by far, and I don't and didn't feel sorry for myself, but that is how I experienced it.

On and off for years, maybe from nine to eleven, I would put myself to sleep praying —yes, I prayed— that my father would be hypnotized and zombie-like would board a ship, out of San Francisco, steam across the Pacific towards China, and —like Winken, Blinken and Nod— would, midway, with the whole ship, drift off planet Earth, sail into space and disappear beyond the moon. And keep going.

JILLIAN (Speechless. Trying to comfort him with her eyes.)

WILLIAM (Calm voice, but the dampening pedal of Calm deepens the message. He waits until the first dampened reverb stops.)

And then it got worse.

JILLIAN (Stunned)

WILLIAM (Glances, reads her) Not now. It's too long, too painful, and too intricate. Some other time. Let my "secrets" ooze out. I'll tell you, but I can't stand to revisit it now. We're having such a good soul-to-soul and if I told you much more your heart would break, and the echoes would depress me for days on and off.

JILLIAN (To gain context, but more to distract and calm herself.) What about Michael?

WILLIAM I'm four years older than him. I was always carrying the sanity football downfield. He could live in my shadow. I ran interference for him. I know that's a mixed metaphor, but you get my point. I was always in the front line of The War. He didn't have to be. But he was behind me completely. At night we'd talk in a whisper. We shared a bedroom.

JILLIAN (Jillian spellbound, visibly sad, almost in tears.) May I ask you one more question?

WILLIAM Yes.

JILLIAN What was your war about?

WILLIAM In a nutshell ...he wanted to drub me into compliance with his delusional worldview. I didn't buy it. I was too independent and, in that way, healthy. I wouldn't join the club. Voluntarily.

JILLIAN How do you know for sure that Michael saw things the way you did?

WILLIAM (Trying to lighten the mood) That's a third question. Anymore, and you'll have to invent a steamy sex scenario and then enact it with me and for me.

JILLIAN Back to point, Sir.

WILLIAM Okay. I'll give you two more "secrets."

Once, when we were at the dinner table, Michael and I —without planning it— started talking gradually softer to make him think that he had really lost his hearing which had started to decline.

JILLIAN (Laughs, in spite of herself, giving in to the sadistic pleasure of the comedy.)

WILLIAM Second one. Once when I was being beaten, with a belt, Michael pretended that the backstroke caught the tip of his penis. I knew he was pretending, and I think our mother did too. She often attended the drubbings. Michael did a good job of acting, holding himself there and crying or pretend crying. My mother reacted by saying to my father, "That's enough. He's had enough".

JILLIAN I can't stand to hear this, it makes me so sad.

If you wish to go on or need to, I'll listen, but you look haggard. And I'm tired and depressed just hearing all this.

WILLIAM (Bright false voice) That's it. I'm finished. An overture. (He exhales decisively. Forced smile.) A few drops syphoned up from my saucer.

JILLIAN (Sees several emotions running through him.) I can see that this takes a lot out of you. (Long hugs him)

WILLIAM That's why I don't talk about it much. Before you and a few other beautiful and wonderful people and things in my life, it was pretty much a downer.

I'll tell you the rest of the essentials some other time, but no one could handle the whole story or stories without going into a depression.

JILLIAN Have you shared the whole story with anyone else?

WILLIAM Over a very long time, with Roberta.

JILLIAN It sounds like she came into your life at just the right time, I appreciate even more the friendship you have with her. ...Would you like a drink of water or to go for a walk?

WILLIAM (Pre-tears in his eyes) Both. A walk. Let's go for a walk.

ACT III

SCENE 5

Two weeks later. A coffee shop, Madison Avenue in the Seventies, Caitlin is already seated. Caitlin gets up. They both hug and kiss, both cheeks, twice, the French way.

JILLIAN Hi. Sorry I'm a little late. Subway delay. I thought it would be faster.

CAITLIN Don't worry about it. What's up?

JILLIAN Let's order first.

(Waitress comes by, they confer and order.)

CAITLIN Tea for her and a coffee for me. And we'll split an apple turnover.

JILLIAN I'm practicing talking like you.

(Both smile)

CAITLIN I'm flattered, I think.

(Both smile again)

JILLIAN ...So, I'll jump right to the point. I asked to talk with you without Roberta so that I could experience you alone.

CAITLIN Good. I am a separate person, you know. (Smiles)

JILLIAN I know that. ...Caitlin, William shared with me that you consciously worked to not fall in love with him. Since we have so many parallels in our past experiences, I feel like we're kindred spirits; so I can't imagine how you didn't fall in love with him. Is there a reason that you didn't or didn't want to?

CAITLIN Wow, you have learned to speak directly! We can't talk about that here. Let's walk over to the Park.

(After finishing their snack, they walk over a few blocks to Central Park, passing the entrance to the Children's Zoo.)

JILLIAN (Out of the blue. Pointing.) Let's sit on one of *those* benches.

CAITLIN Sure. ...You said that funny. Like they hold a special meaning for you, or am I imagining it?

JILLIAN (Laughs) Yes! Good read! Right. I imagine that It's around here, on one of these benches, that Leo and Alma met and talked, and tapped, in the most incredible ending to a novel that I've ever read!

CAITLIN You're *kidding*! Roberta told me —demanded— that I read that book! She and William loved it. More than any other.

JILLIAN Well, love it I do too, although it's not my all-time favorite.

CAITLIN It's not my all-time favorite either. I prefer historical novels. But it was a great book and a very touching ending.

JILLIAN (Mock annoyance) Did they *ever* disagree?

CAITLIN (Mock difficulty, pretend pondering, rubs chin.) Let me think. ...Of course they both love Pink Floyd, but she also loved ELO, the Electric Light Orchestra and he thought they were only so-so, pretty good, not even close to Pink Floyd.

JILLIAN Well *that's* reassuring.

CAITLIN ...In answer to your question at the coffee shop, Jill, there were several reasons.

He liked me or loved me in some ways, I knew that, but Roberta had suggested we date hoping that ...you know....

JILLIAN (Nods)

CAITLIN What I needed was someone who tuned into me as a whole person. He was, essentially, an improvisation coach and a psychotherapist, although we did do the things that lovers do. Our "playtime" made connections happen. Transformation in eighteen "dates," or you could call them, "sessions."

My gratitude to William didn't mean that *I* could see us having a future. *That* magic was not there. Almost, at times, on my side, but only deep affection and happiness on his, not magic.

And of course there's the Roberta factor. They had decided not to marry and to go out with other people. But they still loved each other even if they were not "in" love, and I didn't want to be in a rivalrous position with her, in any way, even potentially.

JILLIAN Thank you. This helps me calm my imagination. I needed this.

CAITLIN (Smiles) You're welcome.

It looks like rain on the way. ...Let's walk back.

ACT III

SCENE 6

Three weeks later. Summer beach cottage of Roberta's friend.

ROBERTA (Big smile) Hello. Welcome to my friend's humble abode. (Hugs, kisses)

JILLIAN Hi. What a cozy place! Nicely decorated. Here, put these in the fridge.

ROBERTA Whatcha got there?

JILLIAN Something for dinner; salad, eggplant parm and a Sauvignon blanc and a Chianti, in case you prefer that.

ROBERTA Well, aren't you the connoisseur?

JILLIAN Trying to be. I prefer whites to reds. You good with it?

ROBERTA Sure. ...But before the sun goes down, let's walk on the beach. You want to change into a bathing suit? My friend's may fit you.

JILLIAN (Smiles) If that's prelude to a seduction, I'm not interested.

ROBERTA (Laughs) No, hon, it wasn't. ...You're funny. You remember things well and you loop back to things. Like William.

JILLIAN (Nods, smiles) In answer to your question, no thanks, but I'd like a sweater or a sweatshirt if she has one that fits. It's cooler than I expected.

I'm so glad you let me come over.

ROBERTA What do you mean "let?" We're friends. I'm delighted that you called to ask, but you have the keys to my kingdom, so to speak. ...Come on now, let your hair down. Would you like something to drink first?

JILLIAN Sure, let's open the white wine. I saw you put it in the fridge, it should be cool now.

As you undoubtedly know, I'm practicing being less filtered.

ROBERTA So I've heard.

(Both smile. After a drink, they exit and walk on the fringe of cool sand. Low tide.)

JILLIAN I want you to know what a deep impression your words made on me. I'm rethinking many things. And I want you to know how grateful I am for your directness. Your courage. (Roberta gestures acknowledgement and smiles.) You probably know that Caitlin and I had a heart-to-heart.

ROBERTA Yes, she told me.

JILLIAN I'd like to know how you got to be so bold, so confident. Did William help you? And did you help him that way?

ROBERTA I've always been this way, mostly, but William helped me tremendously by being a soulmate who I could just talk with, in a totally unfiltered way and get back an honesty level that matched my own. I've never had that completeness with anyone else. Before or since. And I simply love the way he speaks.

JILLIAN I know. ...Roberta, I need you to clarify something. I think I know the answer, but I have to hear your words.

ROBERTA Okay....

JILLIAN I haven't worked out exactly the best way to put this.

ROBERTA Put it un-worked-out.

JILLIAN (Smiles) How can you be so forthright and revealing with me, and not feel a bit uncomfortable? Starting with the day we met?

ROBERTA Jillian, why on earth should I not feel comfortable with you to reveal whatever I wish to reveal? Or not reveal.

JILLIAN You mean you're not this revealing with most everybody?

ROBERTA Of course not! I have boundaries.

JILLIAN Oh.

ROBERTA ...Are you doing a psych eval on me, to see if I'm Borderline or something?

JILLIAN No. Yes. Something like that on myself, actually. I'm trying to shed some of my "internalizations," that I now feel —that you've helped me to see— are ridiculous. But I'm afraid that I might be losing some of my mind, or some of my goodness, some things I like about myself.

ROBERTA Oh, and I'm not kind and generous, as well as self-aware as much as I can be?

JILLIAN Yes, you are.

ROBERTA So? What parts of you are you afraid of losing?

JILLIAN I guess being different. Becoming different from my family and the people I grew up with.

ROBERTA You already are! You're just not ready to accept it. But, even so, let's say you were becoming "different." What bad things are you doing? Have you become selfish, self-centered, unkind, greedy, dishonest, ungenerous?

JILLIAN No.

ROBERTA So, stop it! Redefine what you're going through! You're differentiating yourself into adulthood. And if I may say so —and I base this on what you know I know— you're casting off garbage. You're discarding rubbish from your reference group, including some guys you dated. (Long pause) They didn't deserve you. ...Jillian, you glow so much brighter than you know.

JILLIAN You help me to re-balance, Roberta, thank you.

ROBERTA Jillian, about William, I know his history. He revealed himself to me slowly. Very gradually. His "saucerful of secrets."

What hurt him; how those hurts damaged him; how he thought he would never heal. And how he worked to overcome those things. ...And I know how he loves.

JILLIAN He's told me that he shared his whole story with you, and he's starting to share his history with me. It has so many sad parts. Actually, I'm now glad that he met you because you helped him to repair.

ROBERTA It took a lot of work, but it was a labor of love.

JILLIAN ...But going forward, you haven't said anything about you and him.

ROBERTA ...Jillian, there's another side to all this. Would you want to deprive him of our relationship which is really so much more than physical?

JILLIAN ...I don't know. I'm a very generous person too, but this is exceptional. I might want to restrict him, to see if he loves me enough to live up to it, for me.

ROBERTA So then, you're asking me about the physical side. ...Yes. If you and he want it, then Yes. Consider it *my* first engagement present. Caitlin gave you hers when she retracted her Thank You promise, and I give you this.

JILLIAN I feel six things at once, but mainly, thank you.

ROBERTA Let's head back. We need to eat and just relax.

(Return to cottage)

JILLIAN Roberta, you told me that you love me, or told Caitlin that you were "starting to." I want you to know that I'm "starting to" love you too. (Both smile) And respect you. Very much.

I love seeing you and William interact. How fast it goes and how deep, the mutual respect, and love. I can't say I'll never worry or feel jealous, but I admire it and love it.

ROBERTA Thanks. For all that. You have as much with him. You don't believe it yet, but you will. And —breaking news!— in some ways you have something with him that I don't, and that works for you, with him.

JILLIAN What's that?

ROBERTA I could say, but I won't.

JILLIAN Why not?

ROBERTA Because when you discover it for yourself, it'll be worth a hundred times more than my saying it.

JILLIAN He says that sometimes with his patients.

ROBERTA I know. It's true! (Both smile)

(After dinner, William calls. Roberta puts the call on speakerphone.)

WILLIAM Hi. How's my two favorite people?

ROBERTA and JILLIAN Fine.

WILLIAM Should my ears be ringing?

ROBERTA Sure they should. We talked all about you. *Only* you. (Winks to Jillian) *Non-stop* William.

(Small talk)

ROBERTA You want to drive out and join us for a nightcap?

WILLIAM I'd love to, but I'd love even more to leave you two alone.

ROBERTA Good call. I'd like more time alone with your love-bug.

JILLIAN That's actually good. I'm comfortable and relaxed, and want to get a good night's sleep. I'll call you tomorrow.

WILLIAM When?

JILLIAN After brunch. And maybe a swim.

ALL Bye. Ciao. Bye.

(Curled up on the couch. Leisurely talk about movies, books, friends, some fun times. Share the remainder of the bottle of wine.)

JILLIAN Can I ask you a few things? This is so hard, and I can't believe I'm doing this. I could say it's the wine talking but I really need to know more about this. To understand something.

ROBERTA Well, try me. If I don't want to answer I won't.

JILLIAN Good. That actually reassures me.

ROBERTA Good. Always glad to be *reassuring*.

JILLIAN This is so hard to say. I can't believe what I want to ask.

ROBERTA Ask. (Roberta keeps looking at her, to encourage by waiting.)

JILLIAN Roberta, I want to know more about what your attitude is ...about ...(forces self) with guys you date, ...do you ...blow them?

ROBERTA What!? You mean as standard practice? *No!* Absolutely *not*! Are you kidding me? You're *kidding* me, right?

JILLIAN (Just looks)

ROBERTA It depends! Some No, some, Yes.

JILLIAN Depends. What does it depend on?

ROBERTA It *depends* on what kind of *connection* we have.

JILLIAN Yes?

ROBERTA *Yes*? Of *course*! It depends on how he talks with me ...if we have something emotional or intellectual happening. Both, hopefully. And, if he pays good attention to my body, when I allow that. If I can tell he's seeking to please me, not just warming me up for what he thinks, or hopes, comes next.

JILLIAN You can tell that quickly?

ROBERTA Not *quickly,* Jill, *Instantly*! ...Are you *kidding* me? I monitor my feelings all along the way.

JILLIAN (Breathing hard) Okay. ...Listen ...William told me ...I mean —please forgive me for this ...I asked him— that the first time you and he were together, you blew him.

ROBERTA (Annoyed, but regulating it. Looks hard at her.) You can put it that way, but what are you getting at?

JILLIAN How could you!? I mean ...Why? What I mean is ...

ROBERTA We had a very good connection, Jill.

JILLIAN How did you trust your judgment, so fast?

ROBERTA We were on the same intellectual and emotional level from the get–go. I knew it. He knew it. I read him and he read me and we both knew that we were "reading" each other. Interior stuff. We could tell what the silences between the lines probably meant. We usually got confirmation from the next spoken line.

We had some laughs, but the most important thing was the honesty level. We were immediately able to cross-read each other. I loved that, and he did too. I'd never had it, like that, before. That's what turned me on to him.

(Deliberates. Decides to say it, even though she knows it will hurt Jillian.)

And you should think hard about why you let that happen, did that, without first requiring a real and deep connection.

I'm about the most sex positive person you'll meet, on par with William, but I don't give *anything* away. There has to be a basis. Something reciprocal.

JILLIAN (As if punched in the stomach is unable to take all that in at once. Returns to her focal concern.) And the rest of the physical part?

ROBERTA If I didn't love you I'd never discuss this but since I wish you to be my adopted sister and I know it will help you to make sense of all this, I'll tell you. But I *insist* that you to pay attention to the way I put it. Respectfully. Just like him, when he talks about these things.

JILLIAN I know that now, Roberta. I've grown since our last conversation.

ROBERTA At a certain moment he looked at me and pulled me to him, to kiss. We kissed. Each moment of that makeout session was like a slow-motion tango. Slow. Luxurious. Body–mind connected. No rush. We were registering both ourselves and the other. I realized, very happily, that he was attending to me as much as to himself. He was *in* me, my mind. And we knew it!

I later likened him to an anesthesiologist reading the monitors: heart-rate, O_2, CO_2, breathing pattern, etc.; reading me. It was a double connection. It was a double-consciousness; we felt present inside *both* of our minds at the same time. It was not like sex with other guys. What a powerful turn-on.

JILLIAN That's what I'm having with him, I know, it is very intense. What he taught me. What he insists on.

ROBERTA We did some things —the natural sequence of things you might say— and I could feel his utter enjoyment of me, and *his* registering of *my* enjoyment of what he was doing with me. And please notice, I'm not saying how or where or for how long. It was beautiful. He was in tune with me. I've had that only rarely with others. Every time with him.

JILLIAN I know what you mean. I'm a little jealous hearing this —primitive brain— but also pleased for you, and proud of him.

ROBERTA It was so good, both the conversation and what we did that I thought, "I really want to reward this guy."

JILLIAN So that's when you decided?

ROBERTA Of *course*! You *are* listening to me, aren't you?

JILLIAN (Overwhelmed with all that she has to process can get out only a soft) Yes.

ROBERTA ...Jill?

JILLIAN Yes.

ROBERTA I'm going to tell you two stories.

JILLIAN About him? Him and you?

ROBERTA No. About this topic, and it should help clear up whatever you're working on.

JILLIAN (Completely open) Okay....

ROBERTA I'll make this short. As short as I can. I had been dating this guy. Five or six times maybe. We were at my place, in bed. Fucking. He said, "I want you to blow me."

We were fucking!

I said, "You don't like what's happening?"

He said, "Sure I do. It's just that I want that, too."

I gave him one more chance. Stupidly, he repeated himself. I was furious! "You don't appreciate what we're doing?!" I got him out of me and told him to get out. He said, "What! You can't mean that!" I said, "I do. And I definitely do not want to see you again! Out."

JILLIAN Oh, I love that! I don't think I could ever be so decisive in the moment.

ROBERTA Why not?

JILLIAN How do you do that?

ROBERTA By respecting myself. I honor what my body–mind tallies in the moment. I check myself once, and if I get the same answer, I act.

JILLIAN I was always afraid to hurt their feelings or of losing them.

ROBERTA Right, most girls would give the same answer, but I am not most girls. If a guy is like that, he's not worth my time.

(Pause) Now for the second story. Ready?

JILLIAN (Big breath and release) Yes.

ROBERTA I was going out with someone. A law student from NYU. Maybe it was our second or third date. We were alone at his place. We were making out. A so–so connection, neither good nor bad. There was a little bit of this and that, and then he pushed my head. Down there. I stood up and told him to stand up.

He got up. He must've thought I was going to go down on him like that. I punched him in the mouth! Straight punch. So he had no time to block.

"What's that for?" he said.

"If I want to do that," I said, "you'll know it! Don't you *dare* try to force me to do that!"

"I was encouraging you," he said.

"Fuck you!" I said. "I know the difference between encouraging and forcing!"

Then the savvy lawyer wannabe said, "...You know, I think I'll call the cops on you, for assault."

"Go ahead," I said, "and I'll let them know that you assaulted me by forcing my head down there. And that I was afraid you were going to rape me if I didn't comply. ...How's that?"

He said nothing. He was calculating the case.

"Now call them. Please," I said.

I re-assembled myself and left. That's the only time I've ever hit anyone.

JILLIAN Roberta, you are so strong. I love you for that.

ROBERTA Integrated. Better word. More accurate.

JILLIAN Strong, too.

ROBERTA Strong comes from feeling integrated. I let that guide me. (Gentle smile)

ACT IV

(The Second Expansion)

SCENE 1

Jillian's apartment, several months later. William is there. Enter Roberta, Caitlin and their two friends, Haley and Marcella.

JILLIAN Hello, all. Welcome.

WILLIAM Hello.

ROBERTA Jillian, this is Haley, and this is Marcella. Haley and Marcella, Jillian and William.

HALEY and MARCELLA So nice to meet you.

JILLIAN A pleasure to meet you both.

(All except William take seats, get comfy)

JILLIAN So, how do we all know each other?

HALEY and MARCELLA Well, I met.... (All laugh)

HALEY Roberta is my longtime friend. We were in high school together but had different friends there. We really became friends at my first job when she was working there too, before I went into teaching.

JILLIAN What grades do you teach?

HALEY The hardest ones, they say, Middle School.

JILLIAN Oh, I can easily imagine why they say that.

MARCELLA And I met Caitlin in college. We happened to date the same guy without knowing it.

JILLIAN (Looks toward Caitlin and like she's going to speak)

CAITLIN (Picking up Jillian's glance) No, not at the same time! (Roberta and Caitlin smile. Marcella confused.) We didn't find out about it until a few years later, and then we traded war stories.

(The five women smile)

WILLIAM What say I go out for something to eat? Indian this time? (Jillian, Roberta, and Caitlin laugh)

JILLIAN (To Haley and Marcella) He does this to give us time to womantalk.

WILLIAM So then, that's a Yes? I'll get a mixture of dishes; that way everyone will like something. ...Ciao. (William turns to exit)

JILLIAN (Calling to William at the door) Don't forget the broccoli naan.

(William thumbs-up and exits)

CAITLIN When are your friends coming?

JILLIAN Most likely after lunch. They had errands to run and told me they'd be a little late.

MARCELLA We've only heard about some details. So, there are three bridesmaids?

JILLIAN No. Six. My sister, sister-in-law, and my two friends, and Roberta and Caitlin.

HALEY What color scheme are you thinking about?

MARCELLA Have you picked out your gown?

JILLIAN I am having my gown custom made, I saw the exact one I wanted in the first bridal magazine I bought, and we tailored it for me. I just love it. Here's a photo of my first fitting.

(The women return positive comments. More getting to know you talk and wedding considerations. After an hour William arrives laden with bags, wine, and beer.)

ROBERTA We thought you forgot the address. (Smiles)

WILLIAM I *did.* (All laugh) My radar went down, and I had to ask for directions.

(All sit down to eat. Conversation flows easily. A little while after, Haley and Marcella exit.)

JILLIAN Now that we're alone, do they know anything about you both and him, and me?

ROBERTA No, Jillian. They are just good friends, like anybody has.

CAITLIN What we three have as special friends is precious. Please don't think that we share that with everybody.

ROBERTA When will your friends be here?

(Bell rings. All laugh. Introductions to Jillian's two friends. Small talk, wedding discussion; Roberta and Caitlin exit after a while.)

ACT IV

SCENE 2

Later in Jillian's apartment.

JILLIAN That went well. I get a good vibe from Haley and Marcella. And Roberta and Caitlin seemed to enjoy my friends.

WILLIAM (Smiles) Yep, it was a really nice afternoon. I love watching you interact with people. You're in your element. Jillian, I want you to know, from the bottom of my heart, how happy I am with you. You make me happy.

JILLIAN Thanks. Good. ...but don't get complacent on me.

WILLIAM You really don't have to worry about that.

JILLIAN You'd better live up to that.

ACT IV

SCENE 3

Adirondack, NY, a separate ski chalet associated with a bed and breakfast. Woods, smell of pine, blue jays, squirrels. Jillian and William are on a rare four-day weekend.

JILLIAN (Enjoying her languor. Body and mind relaxed.) I don't know how you do it?

WILLIAM What?

JILLIAN Make love to me morning and night. And sometimes noon too, or at least bring me off if we don't go out.

WILLIAM You still don't know how desirable you are, Silly. How attractive. How sexy. How I want you that much. I want to pleasure you that much. I love to make you come. (Big smile) Simple.

JILLIAN I am one lucky woman.

WILLIAM (Changing direction) I brought some pot. It's supposed to be quite potent. Would you share an experience with me tonight?

JILLIAN Okay. ...I've only tried it twice. And once I got paranoid because I thought people were looking at me thinking "that girl's stoned," and I was afraid I would do something really stupid.

WILLIAM That experience should be done with trusted friends, or alone.

JILLIAN Well then, since you qualify, we'll try it tonight. ...You know, the days are nice and warm, almost hot, but the evenings are chilly.

WILLIAM That's this area and Vermont. I'll use the woodstove when we come back from dinner and the whole place will be toasty. So warm that clothing will be optional. (Big smile)

JILLIAN (Smiles back)

WILLIAM No, on the other hand I love undressing you, piece by piece. Watching you react to my making you increasingly naked in front of me. Watching you as I ravage you with my eyes. I relish it.

JILLIAN (Smiles contentedly) I love it, that you relish and ravage me.

WILLIAM (Big contented smile) If we were in the ice cream business, we'd name a flavor for you, Relished and Ravaged.

JILLIAN (Big smile, picking up on the humor) I'll have some Relished and Ravaged, please. (To William, as if to a server) I'd like to be relished and ravaged, please.

(Smiles, both. Then earnestly.) You should know that I feel that way about you too, and that's the first time in my life that I do. Wholeheartedly.

WILLIAM Ohhh, I love that! You are relished. And you will be ravaged again later. (Big smile)

----- (Hours later, mellow ambiance, blues, jazz and classical music in background, alternately. William returns to living room.)

JILLIAN (Sniffs) Is that it?

WILLIAM Yup. Start small and take gradual tokes ...I'll be right with you all the way.

(Both begin to imbibe through a water pipe, ice water mixed with flavored brandy liqueur to add flavor and aroma.)

WILLIAM (Smiles at Jillian)

JILLIAN This is pleasant. I didn't know you could do it like this. It's mild, not harsh.

WILLIAM Yup. Like me.

JILLIAN (Smiles) Cad!

(Hours pass; they enjoy being high and dancing and singing and generally being silly and sometimes childish again.)

JILLIAN Woooo! I am so tired. Sorry, William, I've just got to go to bed.

WILLIAM Don't feel bad about it. Enjoy it. I'll just fuck you in. Oops, tuck you in.

(Jillian chuckles and returns the smile)

JILLIAN Not tonight. I'm all fuckered out. (Both smile at the wordplay) Good night.

WILLIAM Nightie, night. (Embrace and goodnight kiss) Pleasant dreams.

(Next morning, mid-morning, slow stretches, luxuriously letting their minds awaken, rolling around in bed like kittens. Pillow fighting, play wrestling, kissing and play biting. Rest. Reminiscing leisurely about the experience last night. Then Jillian interrupts, alarmed.)

JILLIAN William!!

WILLIAM Yes. What is it?

JILLIAN I had the *strangest* dream! Strange and *intense*. Oh boy, it was scary too! My heart is racing just remembering it.

WILLIAM Yes?

JILLIAN I know this has meaning, but I'm almost afraid to go there.

WILLIAM What? Let's hear.

JILLIAN I'm in a jungle, South America maybe. In a hut. There's a fire. A *curandero* is walking around with a bowl of something, with some smoke or mist coming off the bowl. He's wearing a loincloth and a headband with feathers in it. He had dark black lines on his cheeks under his eyes. His build was like yours. He sets the bowl on the bare floor. I'm in a hammock. He approaches me. With his eyes he asks me, Where? Where is the pain? I touch my stomach area. He looks at me with penetrating eyes. He turns and picks up the bowl. He offers it to me and gestures me to take a drink and then a big gulp. "Ayahuasca," he says. "Good." "Make good."

Next, what felt like an hour later, he approaches me again and puts his hand into my stomach *through* my skin, and he takes out a balloon half-filled with a whiteish liquid. I awake in the dream and float–walk around the hut and waft outside to look around. Trees. The hut. And float–walk back in, all peaceful. So light. So free. Like healed of something.

WILLIAM (Profoundly touched. Not letting it show in front of her.)

JILLIAN Can you interpret it?

WILLIAM Yes. I don't always think I can, but for certain I know what this means.

JILLIAN Oh, help me to understand it. Tell me what it means. It's important. I sense it.

WILLIAM We'll do it together. I'll do it, *with* you.

JILLIAN Okay.

WILLIAM ...We're away?

JILLIAN Right.

WILLIAM North not south, but that doesn't matter in dreamspace.

JILLIAN Yes.

WILLIAM And the guy reminds you of me and he offers you some drink or smoke. Some "healing smoke."

JILLIAN Yes.

WILLIAM And we're in a hut of a sort. A chalet.

JILLIAN Ohhh, I'm starting to feel something.

WILLIAM What?

JILLIAN *Intense* joy and *intense* shame! Together. It's the *weirdest* combination! It is so intense! ...And now I'm feeling very sad.

WILLIAM Can you get the rest by yourself? (Delays, ponders)

JILLIAN No. My heart is racing. I feel like crying.

WILLIAM Go with it. ...Like the curandero said, "Make good."

JILLIAN I'm afraid. And so sad. (Tears form, no vocals)

WILLIAM Let it happen, Jillian dear. ...What have we been talking about for the last months, aside from everything else?

JILLIAN You telling me that I'm worth more than I've ever felt. (Voice constricting) That I should have been given to....and I shouldn't have ... (Small dry heaves, then more tears and sobbing)

WILLIAM (Let's her sob alone for a time, respecting her private experience, then takes her in his arms and gently rocks in rhythm with her convulsing sobs. ...As she subsides.) Thank you. Thank you so much.

JILLIAN (Wiping her tears) *Me*? Thank you. I thank *you*.

(Begins again to weep, tries to be silent, but very softly sobs audibly. Voice barely above a whisper.) For helping me take away ...you know.

WILLIAM I know.

(Long silence) But it's you that did it. It's your dream. You're healing yourself. You've recognized, and now you can forgive yourself.

JILLIAN I would never have had it without knowing you. Without all that you've given me. (Silence)

Your persistence. Your patience with me. I probably would never have realized what it means. Thank you again. (Hugs him tightly) I don't want to ever let you go. I love you so much.

(Later, after Jillian has settled, William kisses her, from head to toe, no inch unkissed, back and front, and when she is fully kissed, opens and orgasms her orally into oblivion. Oblivion. She sleeps. Then later, that evening, he makes full love to her.)

ACT IV

SCENE 4

William's apartment, a few weeks later.

JILLIAN William....

WILLIAM Uh oh. Whenever you say my name like that, I worry.

JILLIAN I've decided.

WILLIAM Oh good. About?

(Long pause, air pregnant with possibilities)

JILLIAN About my terms.

WILLIAM Terms?

JILLIAN Yes. One thousand days.

WILLIAM ...One thousand days?

JILLIAN I don't want you to be with her or any other woman, for one thousand days.

WILLIAM Uh.... What "be with?" She's a friend. They're friends.

JILLIAN "Be with," as in anything sexual with her or anyone else, from our wedding till then. I want your solemn promise. ...Can you?

WILLIAM Give me a moment! (Long pause) Yes.

JILLIAN Will it be hard for you?

WILLIAM Yes.

JILLIAN Don't just say this, "Yes." It will be a deal-breaker.

WILLIAM Don't even *say* that!

JILLIAN It will really bruise me if you don't live up to it.

WILLIAM I want you to be on solid ground. I will never lie to you. I want you to feel secure.

(Returning to his ironic stance) It's only three years.

JILLIAN (Jillian ignoring the humor, scans him like a mother trying to make a child feel guilty, to test the child, even if she knows he has done nothing wrong.) From our wedding. "Talk with."

WILLIAM You won't be jealous–fearful if I contact them as friends?

JILLIAN Not if you give me no reason to fear. And if you don't change towards me. Either our love will succeed and grow, or it will fail. I will trust our fate.

WILLIAM Thank you for that! Thank you for being willing to trust me that much.

JILLIAN And what's more, ...I'm putting restrictions on you.

WILLIAM Oh god, I've taught you too well.

JILLIAN Be quiet! Just relax.

WILLIAM I am tame.

JILLIAN (Snickers at the wording) If you live up to it ...if you live up to having nothing physical with her for one thousand days —and if I have no doubts about it— then I will reward you.

(Slight, inscrutable smile) ...Magnificently.

WILLIAM (Silent, not knowing where this might go, tension palpable)

JILLIAN (Very long pause)

WILLIAM The suspense! Please Jillian, what?

JILLIAN If you do that and if I have not a shadow of doubt —not one— then....

WILLIAM Yes...?

JILLIAN (Hesitating, deciding whether or not to utter the words....) I will permit you, twice per year....

WILLIAM (Stunned. Pleased. Speechless.)

JILLIAN But I want to know about it, if it happens. I want to know all about it! And whoever they are, they must meet all appropriate requirements, of course, meaning, the same restrictions as yours.

WILLIAM (Tries to regulate his breath, and smiles.)

JILLIAN (Watches as he struggles to process it all; what it means for her, for him.)

WILLIAM (Deep, quiet voice) You knock me out! You take my breath away. ...Thank you.

JILLIAN Is that a promise?

WILLIAM Yes. Promise. Or you can punish me.

JILLIAN Oh, don't worry, I will. Grievously!

(Both laugh)

And no cadettes in training!

ACT IV

SCENE 5

Jillian's apartment, a few days later. Lying in bed, pillow talking.

JILLIAN William....

WILLIAM Yesss....

JILLIAN (Giggles) I've been thinking. What will you do when Roberta marries?

WILLIAM (Blinks!)

JILLIAN You haven't thought of that?

WILLIAM Yes. No. I mean of course I have. I block it, I put off thinking about it.

JILLIAN I get that.

WILLIAM I'll be very happy for her, truly. But it's an unpleasant thought to relinquish being her most trusted person.

JILLIAN All of our relationships will change.

WILLIAM I know. (Finding his balance. Lovingly busting her.) How did you get to be so damned smart? I want to keep my friendship with her, especially our sister–brother communication.

JILLIAN I know. But there will be the matter of who her husband is. What he'll be like.

WILLIAM I know.

JILLIAN He might pick up on the effortless rapport you two have —I'm talking mentally-emotionally— and discourage the relationship because he's afraid of it. Even engineer to ruin it.

WILLIAM I know. But I've met some of the guys she's dated, and had an easy initial rapport with them. I really don't think that Roberta would marry a guy who wouldn't respect our relationship.

JILLIAN Yeah, but I can also picture a guy loving her so much that he would jealously guard her. He'd wonder if there had been more to the relationship that he doesn't know about. Do you think you're the only one who picks up under–harmonics so acutely?

WILLIAM No.

JILLIAN An inadvertent look, or a too–quick response, could send the partner down a paranoid path. Remember what your patient said, 'Just because I'm paranoid, doesn't mean they're not all out to get me.'

WILLIAM (Chuckles) I know. That's a great line, and true some of the time!

JILLIAN I would occasionally be conflicted relating to him.

WILLIAM Why?

JILLIAN Well, ...I might want to say something more but be afraid that her husband would think, later on, that there might be a second meaning to what I said, which it might. ...Or that I seemed to know his wife exceptionally well. Too well, and wondered how. Even from a joke.

WILLIAM This is all supposition, over-thinking. It could all work out.

JILLIAN I know. It could. I hope it doesn't change too much.

(Pause) I want only you William. I always will. I know it. I want you to want only me, but I get you now. I understand you. Enough to give you my magnificent gift —if you live up to it I remind you— but, if and when she's married....

WILLIAM (Stroking her face with his hand) Jillian, it didn't escape me that in your magnificent gift you had neither included nor left out Roberta. I love you for that. You left it open for me to decide. A double gift. (Kisses her)

I have been soul-searching. Quite frankly, the way Roberta and I are constituted, we could be in our own loving relationships, be fully respectful of them, and yet enjoy each other fully without marring those relationships. But, while I know that she and I could do that, I want you to fully enjoy a relationship with Roberta and not have it tinged with thoughts of Roberta and me sexually. I so enjoy seeing the friendships grow between you and her, and you and Caitlin. I want them to grow. I want to foster them in any way I can.

Also, I've never wanted to be with a woman behind her husband's back. I'm not looking for an Oedipal victory.

So ...for all those reasons, I will match your gift in kind. I will not have intimate relations with Roberta going forward.

JILLIAN (Swallows hard and whispers) Thank you.

(Very nice voice, gently mischievous) You'll just have to find replacements. (Smiles)

WILLIAM (No words. Face groans then morphs into a complex smile. Sequence: first sad at the prospect, then pleased that Jillian can offer or hint this, if it is a real offer, then delighted that she can represent his future choices so non-hostilely!)

JILLIAN (Smiles back, reading his sequence)

WILLIAM *(She's reading me. And she knows I know why she's smiling.)*

JILLIAN Yes. (*Without* supplying what she is saying 'Yes' to)

WILLIAM You look like a possum, smiling like that!

(Both crack up at this echo)

JILLIAN I know.

(Second wave of smiling and laughing, now with an undercurrent of sadness.)

WILLIAM (Again, *She knows I know why she's smiling*)

JILLIAN (Smiles back) Yes. (Smiles back, *again* without supplying what she's saying 'Yes' to)

ACT IV

SCENE 6

Next morning, sitting on her balcony having breakfast.

JILLIAN You know, last night was so beautiful. We spoke so honestly that it released an inhibition in me.

WILLIAM Really? What?

JILLIAN What if you couldn't accompany me to a conference, or I'm in Italy visiting friends —say twenty years from now— and I want to be with somebody, a one night stand ...what would you say to that?

WILLIAM (Not believing what he's being asked and knows that he must answer honestly and not be roundabout) ...I wouldn't like it.

...But after that long, if you needed or wanted re-affirmation that way, from another source, to prove something to yourself, I'd understand it. ...You've promised me so much freedom, I'd have to not stand in your way. I'd wouldn't like it, but I'd endure it. To be fair.

JILLIAN (Not relenting. Her eyes penetrating his.) And the other "thing?"

WILLIAM. Jillian, we've actually had this conversation before.

JILLIAN No we haven't! What conversation? We've never talked about this. I'm not forgetting.

WILLIAM Yes we have, in my mind. This is a "secret" I've never told to you.

JILLIAN What! Why not?

WILLIAM Because I didn't want you to have an easy way out.

JILLIAN Out of *what*? What easy way? What are you *talking* about?

WILLIAM Our relationship.

JILLIAN What!? Come on. Spit it out!

WILLIAM (Softly, slowly, funereally.) If you *ever*, so much as kiss another man's penis, or balls, *let alone* ...suck another man's cock, *let alone* ...give him head to make him hard and ready him to come, and *worst* ...let him come in your mouth, and *worse than worst* ...swallow it ...our relationship would be over. Done. Shattered. A death-ray.

You'd have put a needle in the brainstem of our relationship! All the king's men and all the king's horses couldn't put Humpty Dumpty back together again.

JILLIAN (Stunned at the ferocity of his decisiveness. Happy, because she truly never wishes to do that with anyone other than him anyway. Confused, by the fairness argument. Gathers herself.)

What if I felt that way? And isn't that similar to your Ex-?

WILLIAM First question first. You are different than me. Our whole story would be different if you felt that way. We certainly wouldn't be where we are.

Still on your first question in wider focus: I've proven myself to you over and over. In spades. How much I love you and how I love.

JILLIAN Meaning? ...The last part?

WILLIAM Meaning that I was never distracted while our love was growing even with Roberta and Caitlin lightly sprinkled in the background. ...Would you have believed that *that* was possible when we first met? If you had known beforehand?

JILLIAN No! I would have thought you were a jerk, and I wouldn't have gone out with you.

WILLIAM Right. But they've proven out ...in ways similar to how I'm proving out. You didn't expect that. Rather, the opposite. But you let yourself experience them for who they are, and you've grown to respect them. You know how society would judge them. You did, originally ...think them a kind of prostitute. You know them well now and you respect them, even love them!

Jillian, I've told you. You are different. Your essence charmed me. We are different, essentially. There are some women —not many— Roberta, or Edna O'Brien or Colette, for others, who are like me.

JILLIAN *Edna, Colette*, who are *they*!! Other *"friends"* of yours?

WILLIAM (Laughs) No. They're writers. An Irish writer and a French one. Beautifully liberated people. But let's keep on track. Like them, I exist in my unique ways. And my escapades will be few and far between. (Catches his breath while she is absorbing)

And to anticipate you, what all women worry about *won't* happen with us. I will not "trade you in for a newer model." I don't think like that. When I love, I love deeply. Indelibly. You have proof of that. I will prove out long-term.

...And now to your second question....

JILLIAN (Quick smile) I'm glad you remember it. Not pretending that you forgot it, as you've done sometimes.

WILLIAM (Remembers. Returns the smile.) No, I'm *not* like my Ex-.

Proof? Unpleasant as the prospect is to me, I give you permission. 'Twenty years from now.' If your need at that point mirrors mine. How could I block you?

...And how many guys would do that? How many husbands could even *hear* the words? Even *consider* it? And, for the woman who dared utter those words to half the males in the world I would expect dire consequences! Physical.

(Holds her eyes) I can identify with you that strongly, even if I'd hate the idea. I *am* fair.

JILLIAN Hon, out of respect for you and your Ex-, I've never asked you for any details. You rarely speak of her and then only vaguely. But I want you now to confide something essential about the two of you and what went wrong.

WILLIAM Okay. I will. Indulge me for a moment. Let me set this up right. You know how I think. Let me "walk you around the corner, and then bring you back."

JILLIAN (Slight frown with almost a smile)

WILLIAM I once had at the same time four couples in treatment who were close to contemplating divorce proceedings. On the weekend prior to seeing them next, I happened to meditate on them and their situations. I concluded that two of the couples might make it and two would not. I made a bet with myself.

Four for four. I was wrong about all of them! Those who I thought *might* work it out, didn't, and those who I thought would *never* reconcile, did.

JILLIAN What made the difference?

WILLIAM The difference was that some of the "aggrieved" parties —gender doesn't matter, it was two women and two men— could *imagine* forgiving.

The others could not. Simple as that. That's just who they were, how they were constructed, their bottom line. It was outside the solar system of their imaginations. No fault of their own.

I learned something from being so drastically wrong. This issue is not fungible. It's like being pregnant; you can't be both not and pregnant at the same time. If they couldn't imagine it, it was a dead issue.

My Ex- was of the latter construction. I went from being Wonderful Lover, Best Friend, Honest Interactor, sometimes Intellectual Guide, Father-to-be of any future child or children, to Scumbag, Louse, Liar, Traitor and Loser. Scumbag of the first degree!

JILLIAN Did you try to change?

WILLIAM Yes, but ultimately it didn't matter.

You know I sometimes joke about how much I admire aspects of Chinese and Japanese culture that I'm "planning to go in for an operation to become Chinese...."

JILLIAN (Annoyed at the delay, but then with a slight smile knowing he will get back to the point.) Yes....

WILLIAM Well, I can have epicanthal folds made for my eyes, but I can't become Chinese, gene-wise.

JILLIAN Clarify please. You swoop too fluidly from abstract to concrete and back again that we John Q. Public ordinary folks can't follow sometimes.

WILLIAM Ground level: I could not promise, without lying, that for the rest of my life I would never seek pleasure and affirmation and whatever else it is about me, with another woman. I didn't want to lie. And we knew each other too well; she would have known it.

No matter how many screens a woman would have had to pass so that we —she and I— did not have to worry, no matter how infrequent, no matter how discretely done, the answer was categorical.

I loved her and was totally satisfied with her. It would have taken one heartbeat for me to choose to die for her to save her life. But try as I did, I couldn't prevent the yearnings. Not that I did anything about them, but the beast wouldn't sleep.

And for her, the beast of feeling obliterated could not be subdued, even though in my opinion, she had no valid reason to feel that way. I changed *nothing* in the way I treated her and felt about her. But *that*, as she pointed out, was how I felt about it. For her, it was categorical. And then, naturally, our sex life suffered. So the healing avenue of intimacy was blunted. I had become garbage, and everything about me was too. My good points didn't matter.

Some people are that way. The majority probably. In our culture. They are no more capable of changing that than I am capable of becoming Chinese, even with surgery. (She smiles)

It's a self-esteem thing massively reinforced by the prevailing culture, and sometimes also from the family-of-origin story.

(Half talking to himself) And how long did it take for everything to be overthrown? Newton's formula: $\frac{1}{2}gT^2$: solve for Time. It took three seconds for everything —our history, my love— to be jettisoned. I was pushed out of a plane without a parachute. Free-fall. Splatter.

And I respect that she felt shattered too. I don't hate her and in fact still have a tiny tender spot for her even though I know she'd prefer me dead.

We couldn't help it. It was just who we were.

...Love conquers all? Sometimes. Not always.

JILLIAN How sad. ...Thank you. ...It must have taken you a long time to recover.

WILLIAM (Recovering his capacity for irony, light tone.) Only half a decade. (Then serious and sad.) Yes. You bet. That's why I want to get all this right between us. Why I've insisted on you knowing me down to my core.

...When she said that about my hurts, my belief that I would never heal, my efforts to overcome those hurts and heal myself, this is what Roberta was referring to.

Jillian, you've told me that you know you'll want me always and you'd like me exclusively, permanently. You've also come to understand me as the person that I am. And you've given me the gift of rare occasional playtimes. I won't abuse that privilege. I cherish you even more for that! I love you at yet another level for that. Your gift bonds me to you even tighter.

We love children in different ways because they're different individuals. You and I are different. We're composed differently. We're different substances. What we're hashing out is how to best satisfy ourselves *and* keep the sacredness of our upcoming marriage. To expect everyone to fit the same mold is stupid. Even cruel. An argument based on simpleminded "equality" is irrelevant and demeaning.

...I am and will be faithful to you, in the way that you're trying to grant. We can go around and around trying to nuance this more, but the bottom line is what I've already said.

JILLIAN That was put so thoughtfully and beautifully. We are very different. I enjoy our differences. I've done a lot of soul searching too. I want to see you happy in your life with me and not feel caged. You've helped me to appreciate that not everybody falls into a standard form and that doesn't make them automatically bad or weird or despicable. I trust that you will keep me central and I will live on that trust.

WILLIAM (Reaches for her, kisses her) Thank you.

ACT V

(The Engagement)

SCENE 1

Engagement party: Central Park; the locale reminiscent of Seurat's, Sunday Afternoon on the Island of La Grande Jatte. A beautiful, mild autumnal day. Blue sky. Trees in the distance with leaves in orange, burgundy, yellow and brown frame the celebrants. The still green lawn serving as a mat for the picture.

Jillian, William, Roberta, Caitlin, Haley, Marcella, two other friends of Jillian's, her brother and sister-in-law, her sister, and William's two friends, David and Charles, and his brother, Michael.

WILLIAM A toast! What a perfect afternoon. And it's more perfected by having all of the people I most love all around me. Thank you for sharing your time and love with Jillian and me. Thank you for being here.

JILLIAN Thank you. I can't tell you how much it means to me to be surrounded by your love.

ROBERTA Are honored guests allowed to propose toasts too?

(All laugh) ...I have to say how thrilled I am to be taken as a sister by Jillian. William I already knew, he is like a brother to me, and I could not have wished a more suitable mate for him than you, Jillian. Here's to you both! Long live our friendship and love.

CAITLIN God, you say things so well sis! (All laugh) I wish you the same, Jillian and William. You both are amazing people and your love for each other is amazing. It's something we all see and feel. Thank you for allowing us to share in it.

DAVID And we hope to give you all the love we can. Not hope! Intend! We want to make your lives happy and fulfilled. You have enriched ours so much.

CHARLES You are not my older brother, David, (All laugh) but I could not have said that better. (All laugh again) William and Jillian, we bask in the reflected sunshine of your love and we will be there to support you both.

(Cheers, all around. Glasses lift.)

MICHAEL I am, in fact, Bill's younger brother, (All laugh) and I'm not known for eloquence. For conciseness maybe, but eloquence, not. All I can say is, Jillian, thank you for bringing my brother happiness.

ACT V

SCENE 2

Same place, wider angle, middle-distance view. A figure walks toward the engagement party from a nearby tree. With the sun glare, it's hard to tell who it might be. It is a woman.

WILLIAM (Blanches) How th...!

(All murmur, trying to make sense of the sharp change of mood.)

CHARLES It's his Ex-.

(The tableau freezes. The only thing moving, the figure proceeds into their circle.)

FIGURE (Advancing. Pleasant voice.) Hi Bill.

(Flicks a glance to the side.) Your trained monkeys?

(Advances) Your coven of bitches?

(Advances. Voice still controlled.) Do you think you deserve to have all this happiness?

(Advances, opens her handbag, nice voice.) I don't.

(Takes a pistol from her handbag. Fires point blank. William falls dead on the spot, a bullet through his heart.)

(Screams, confusion.)

(Figure walks calmly away towards the periphery of the park. Not caring, knowing that she will be eventually apprehended.)

SOMEONE Ohhhh! Oh god! Is he alive?
SOMEONE Call the police.

SOMEONE This can't be!

SOMEONE Jillie's collapsed.

SOMEONE What should we do?! Is he alive?

ROBERTA (Goes to help her, to hold her.)

DAVID Call an ambulance!

SOMEONE Why would anyone do this?

SOMEONE Oh, Poor Jillie.

SOMEONE What should we do?

SOMEONE A train of monkeys?

SOMEONE Call a doctor!

MICHAEL I'm a doctor.

SOMEONE Is she crazy?

SOMEONE Get an ambulance.

SOMEONE Call the police.

SOMEONE What "witches?"

SOMEONE Should we stop her?

DAVID Poor Jillian. Oh, poor Jillian.

ROBERTA Oh god. Poor Jillian.

HALEY All our hearts crack as one. Ohhhhhh. Ohhhhhh...

Notes

Keywords or equivalents:

bold, (boldly, boldness, blatantly)

documentation, (check, cross-check, vetting)

exuberance

transactionally

Part 3

The Confession

Introduction [3a]

Appearing, like a combination of Mr. Magoo and Moses–with–the–tablets, Professor Morton Seiden wafted into the classroom, managed to guide the books he was carrying into a controlled tumble onto the desk, squinted and thereby deftly rearranged slightly the glasses on his nose without use of hands, peered through his glasses, looked out the window in the back of the room to gaze at the one tree offering a natural respite, and, centered himself. Then, without so much as glancing at the plebes crammed into the room and as if addressing a convocation of Pulitzer or Nobel peers, intoned: "In 1922, Joyce's *Ulysses* was published, and nothing in literature has been the same since. Its impact was epoch–changing, like that of Picasso's painting fifteen years earlier, and anyone writing since has been influenced by it either directly or at the very least has felt its impact by reflection." Thus spoke the demi-god of Modern British and American Literature exposition. *Also Sprach Zarathustra*? *Also Sprach Morton Seiden*.

In another class I learned that dialog and action were everything for narratives and drama, especially dialog in drama. So, from this four-decade remove, I recall, clear as a bell, how he began deconstructing *Macbeth*, through the keywords, "red," "blood," "bloody," and "incarnadine." Still clear.

And *Hamlet*, through the changes of perspective that the characters go through —most of all Hamlet's changes, recognizing near the end that, "readiness is all." Meaning, that being in the moment as well as being willing to act is 'all.' Experience–Integrate–Act, not over-filter.

In dialog, characters must sound like themselves and must be identifiably different from each other. The main characters must evolve. The storyline must flow. And, if possible, the ending must not be predictable. Ideally, the author must have no discernible axe to grind. Will Shakespeare's axe has not been found in four hundred years of searching for it. Genius.

I remember a dream that William told me about. Unforgettable. Mid-seventies. He walked into a party and, front and right, there was Roger Waters! He didn't want to bother him, but also didn't want to waste the opportunity, to thank him from the bottommost part of his heart, for what David Gilmour and he had done in creating *Celestial Voices*, the turbulent, triumphant, ecstatic whirlpool ending of *A Saucerful of Secrets*. He was speechless, all he could finally get out was, "How did you get the courage to be that honest?"

I thought a lot about that dream for years afterwards. William's writing was that courageous. I decided that if I *ever* wrote, I would have to equal William's courage and also be as courageous as David and Roger were, vocally and musically, in *Celestial Voices*. That would be *my* standard. I would have to be as emotionally honest and naked as they were.

Believe me, I have had to summon Courage to let his work stand as it is, to let us be known emotionally stark naked. I might have prevailed on him to change the names, our names, but you would have uncovered *that* fig leaf. You cannot know *exactly* what was fiction and what fact, so, intuit what you will, that blend is yours. I've struggled to let the work stand as it is. I entertained the ruse of a fig leaf. But no, it had to be this honest. This *is* how we spoke to each other and those *were* the issues we wrestled with.

I, Jillian, did not write *The Walrus*.

William wrote it. It was his: conception, gestation, and almost-delivery. I am but the last-minute doula. Being dead, William could no more have written the ending to Act V, Scene 2, than Hamlet could have written the ending to *Hamlet*. Everything was his, except the few words at the very end.

For that matter, he couldn't he have written Act V, Scene1. I wrote it! I had to. I was there. As close readers, think about it. When I came to from my faint, my head was cupped in Roberta's hand, nestled on her thigh. Her other hand was stroking my head and face. Tears streamed down her face. I heard the voices. My eyes still closed, I recognized Michael's voice and David's, and I heard the others. I heard Haley howl. I could supply the ending, so I have. I have patched together who said what, as best I can.

With this I am making amends for provisionally putting my name on *The Walrus*. For commandeering it. I am offering amends. I am guilty exactly like Zvi and Rosa Litvinoff, but unlike them, I am truly contrite. I offer full restitution to you with this, now. I misled you. I let you and my six readers believe it was mine. That I had invented a story, or transmuted my story or parts of it, into art. Yes, I had a hand in it, but only the tiniest part, more like a finger, more like a fingernail, more like a clipping from the pinky of the non-dominant hand.

I, who have been so honest about everything else in my life, blinked. I so wanted another soul whose mind could wrap around me and nourish my soul like William's did, that I blinked. I was afraid, Morton, that you would lose interest in me if I did not have writing in common with you. I couldn't tell you. Then. But now is now.

Stay with me.

Morton, from him and you, I got the real start of my mind. From you: What is a novel? a short story? a play? a screenplay? a prose poem? an essay? How are they different? Are the boundaries fixed or permeable?

Can a Work work that is all of these and none alone?

A desire was born in me to test the limits of these definitions —if I even *had* the capacity to write, anything, or ever wrote at all. Why? Obviously, to intrigue and surprise you. To show you what I am capable of and maybe gain your admiration. But it is this, *this* this, not *The Walrus*, that is my Work. You will see and understand shortly, very shortly.

Years later, after the tragedy, you said to me that *The Walrus* broke all the rules; and that you loved it. Not for the rule-breaking, but because it worked. It flowed. You compared it to a tarte, "crisp and crunchy heavy, alternating with smooth and creamy light." And that you loved the abrupt ending. "I didn't anticipate it." On a praise scale of one–to–ten that was a ten. I accepted it silently, on William's behalf. An honorarium to him, from one he honored. Morton, this is my bequest to you.

My Confession [3b]

Morton's apartment, Brooklyn Heights. A home health aide is seen exiting the room, while the dogwalker is putting a leash on a large black standard poodle to go out for a walk. Morton and Jillian have been reminiscing.

MORTON: ...and Haley and Marcella, such a nice touch. Horatio and Marcellus. (Chuckles) And Roberta being the one to go to Jillian, to comfort her. That was a such a lovely touch! Just right.

JILLIAN: You nailed it. Then and now. As I thought you would.

MORTON: As you hoped I would, you mean. (Jillian laughs lightly) If I still had my marbles. (Both laugh) It has been a few years.

JILLIAN: That did cross my mind. (Both laugh)

MORTON: And the whole play turning on the word, "transactionally." And her growth doubly dramatized in the dream scene! Now *that* was wonderful!

JILLIAN: (Reacting, head nodding up and down, deeply grateful but also hiding her shame, speechless for a while.) Thank you. Thank you for getting it, the first time, and now.

MORTON: Enough already. I'll get a big head.

JILLIAN: Your recognition means so much to me. And would have meant so much to William. That's exactly what he said (Covering gesture) ...would have said.

MORTON: What do you mean? I'm not following. When did he say that?

JILLIAN: I missed a beat. (Fumbling, trying to recover) I mean about the word, "transactionally," being central. (Realizing that she is overwhelmed, going to reveal too much too soon) I'm sorry. I don't know. My lapse. I think I had a senior moment. I overlap the two of you at moments. Forgive me. You both mean so much to me. What I think I meant was that that's why he put the Notes in after the play. (Catching herself again, covering) I mean talked me into putting them there.

MORTON: What? Are you going daffy on me? Don't be going daft, Jillian. Two codgers confused at the same time makes not for coherent conversation.

JILLIAN: (Laughs at the wording, recovers) I won't. It's Okay, I'm back.

MORTON: You're back. You sure?

JILLIAN: I'm sure.

MORTON: (Letting that go) I didn't read your work just once, Jillian. I read it more than once. Many, many times, actually. And I re-read it in the run-up to this rendezvous. You created a very intricate work. Yet it flows. Congratulations. (Big smile) Again.

JILLIAN: Thank you again Morton. I'll stop, but I want you to know how relieved and gratified I am. (Truthful, and at the same time covering) For William, too, I mean, (Covering) he would have been so proud (one millisecond blip) of me.

MORTON: (Ignoring the blip and returning to the business at hand) I really loved the dream scene. I am very proud of you.

JILLIAN: (Sighs, head down) Thanks.

MORTON: (Pause) You know ...I could justify an argument that *The Walrus* should be considered a prose poem as much as a play. The verbal latticework is filigreed to that extent. ...Or a verbal symphony, with the bass lines —what you call the under–harmonics— carrying a rhythm under the melody of the action. Congratulations again! Really.

JILLIAN: It wasn't that hard, really.

MORTON: You've got to be *kidding*! Why are you being so overly modest?

JILLIAN: I just—

MORTON: Stop!

JILLIAN: Yes. Thank you.

MORTON: (Nods acceptance and returns to the literary business) To quote myself, (jokingly), you have a future in this field if you want it. (Coaxing chuckle)

JILLIAN: I've had a gratifying career in the field of my choice, thank you very much. You know that.

(Fishing for a way to start revealing, but still trying to cover)

I loved creating this once I started it, but, you know my field has been elsewhere.

MORTON: "This?" Did you say "this?" *What* "this?" Did you mean, "that" or "it?"

JILLIAN: (Covering) It. (Backpedaling, not wanting to lie) Did I say 'this?' Senior moment number two. Sorry. *Culpa mea.*

(Long pause. Silence. Each sip tea slowly, each sensing mood.)

JILLIAN: Morton, do you still read?

MORTON: Yes, if you can call it that. Why?

JILLIAN: I just want to know. Your whole career was literature. Can you still?

MORTON: Sort of. My vision works ...better than my dick.

JILLIAN: (Both snicker-laugh) Stop it, Morton. You're making me uncomfortable.

MORTON: I am tame. (Both smile at the quote) I just like to remember when I had one, that's all. It's not everyone I can be naughty with.

JILLIAN: You gestured over there.

MORTON: Yes. To your question, with the help of that thing. (Gestures to a high-intensity lamp with a built-in magnifier.) It's slow going, but yes, slowly.

JILLIAN: Slow is good. Better, sometimes. Like naughty. (Both laugh, lightly, Morton not quite sure.)

MORTON: What is the real subject of our conversation at this moment? Are you shadow-playing?

JILLIAN: (Diverting) I'm concerned, eager to know if you still enjoy reading.

MORTON: Hmmm. And that's all?

JILLIAN: Yes, Silly.

MORTON: Are you not getting at something else?

JILLIAN: (Evading) I'm so glad. At least it's something.

MORTON: Jillian ...methinks you fish for something.

JILLIAN: (Laughs, slightly embarrassed, laughs again) Maybe.

MORTON: Don't be coy.

JILLIAN: (Covering and diverting, but also honestly asking.) Morton, I'd love to know your favorite novel of the last hundred years.

MORTON: (Allowing himself to take the bait and letting Jillian escape, perhaps temporarily.) Oh, only that? One?

JILLIAN: How many do you need?

MORTON Ten. Twenty. Only the best!

JILLIAN: No, seriously. I want only your all-time favorite one, ...or two.

MORTON: I am serious.

JILLIAN: How about two?

MORTON: Okay, then ...two. (Teasingly) Not three? I could give you the first five without thinking about it.

JILLIAN: (Laughs) Okay, then, two. (Both laugh)

MORTON: Sure?

JILLIAN: Sure.

MORTON: (Playing, by mildly torturing her) Sure?

JILLIAN: Yes. (Laughs) Please, I'm sure. Go on.

MORTON: Make it the best of the last fifty years? One hundred would be too many.

JILLIAN: Okay, then.

MORTON: If I have only two, I don't even have to think about it.

JILLIAN: Yes ...? You're *torturing* me.

MORTON: John Fowles', *The Magus,* and Nicole Krauss', *The History of Love.*

JILLIAN Wow! Why them?

MORTON: Because Fowles dramatizes the ...the ...the, what is the word?

JILLIAN: Do you mean...

MORTON: Quiet Jill! I will get it! Let me have peace!

JILLIAN: I am tame, sir. Pronounce.

MORTON: (He laughs, then Jillian does, then both laugh) You remember that that well?

JILLIAN: Yes. 3:2. You taught me to remember things that way! (So as not to tease him) Act 3: Scene 2.

MORTON: What?

JILLIAN: Act 3: Scene 2

MORTON: What!

JILLIAN: (Signing to Morton to adjust his hearing aid, then reaching over and putting his hand to one ear.)

MORTON Oh, yes. Damned things!

JILLIAN: (Smile, soft comforting)

Morton: Don't get old, Jillie.

JILLIAN: Okay, I won't. (Both laugh; her laugh turning to softly bitter at the end)

MORTON: First, my feet got cold. And stayed cold! (Pause) Then my dick stopped working. (Jillian is mildly embarrassed. He senses her embarrassment.) What? I don't have one?

JILLIAN: (Embarrassed now at her embarrassment, laughs.) Yes, yes of course. (Stops short)

MORTON: Or had one. ...What was I saying?

JILLIAN: You were giving me the short list.

MORTON: Of what?

JILLIAN: Of the slings and arrows that outrage your body.

MORTON: (Glances at her but chooses not to pick up on the reference) Then my hands got cold and mostly stay that way. I think only my heart and my brain keep plugging along, and one of them not always at full capacity.

JILLIAN: With half a brain, Morton, your mind is more vivid than most.

MORTON: Thanks. (Real chuckle, then turns bittersweet) Now, what did you say?

JILLIAN: I had said, Act 3: Scene 2.

MORTON: Of what!

JILLIAN: I had said, "I am tame, sir. Pronounce." ...From *Hamlet*.

MORTON: Oh, yes. (Laughs) (Both laugh) Of course. (Pause) Jillie, you are a beautiful mind.

JILLIAN: Oh, (minimizing tone) I was taught by a god.

MORTON: Oh, good. That's good! (Pause) ...This god, is he available for worship by me too?

JILLIAN: (Draws breath)

MORTON: (Before she can respond) And does he intervene! *That* is the question! I need a boatload of intervention. (Both laugh)

JILLIA: Well, it happens that he *is* available.

MORTON: (Draws breath)

JILLIAN: (Before he can speak, teach-ish mock seriously) Simply 'govern these ventages...' (both laugh, knowing that this was a setup distractor, she restarts) Simply give obeisance to your reflection when it looms in the mirror.

MORTON: (He laughs again) Yeah, right.

JILLIAN: Even if it is hazy in spots. (Both laugh, turns somber)

MORTON: Jillian, you have developed a wry sense of humor. Wickedly wry.

JILLIAN: Wicked is good sometimes, too. (Both laugh) Like naughty. (Both laugh again)

MORTON: Yes, naughty is good. By the way, how do you do that?

JILLIAN: What?

MORTON: Remember. So specifically.

JILLIAN: Someone taught me.

MORTON: Oh yes? May I know who?

JILLIAN: Morton, ...*you* taught me!

MORTON: *I* did? How?

JILLIAN: You remember, one time when I came to your office for help framing some project? Maybe it was the second or third time. I wanted suggestions. To organize the parts of it.

MORTON: (Exaggerates) Me remember? (Exaggerates again) No. (Both laugh) Vaguely, vaguely.

JILLIAN: You told me that I must learn to command my mind. You said, "You have to govern it. The "ventages" are connected by associations. You must learn to govern them. Demand your mind to make connections!"

MORTON: That sounds great, but how? ...Did I really?

JILLIAN: You said that I should pick my two, or max three, favorite lines in a play or story and command myself to say what scene or page it's on. Over and over, until I memorized the association and didn't have to think about it any longer. For two or three weeks. A mantra, and then I'd have it.

MORTON: I said that?

JILLIAN: Yup. You did. You want more examples?

MORTON: You expect me to say No, so I'll say Yes.

JILLIAN: (Going with his oppositional feint rather than opposing it.) You said it didn't have to be literature: Newton's five papers,1667; Einstein's five papers, 1905; The Federalist Papers, #43, Madison, on factions; Chomsky, *The Managua Lectures*, page 159.

MORTON: Brilliant. I must have been brilliant. (Both laugh) Operative words: "have been."

JILLIAN: (Smiling, purposely underplaying her agreement) It worked for me.

(Pause, both take sip or two of tea)

Morton: I remember something. (Stalling)

JILLIAN: (Exaggerating surprise, teasing mildly) You do? Very good.

MORTON: (Pretend anger) Stop that! (Then smiling) We were talking about something. What were we talking about? You know, before that.

JILLIAN: Uhm. You had silenced me and wanted time to recall a word, a concept.

MORTON: Sounds like me. About what?

JILLIAN: About why *The Magus* is so great and

MORTON: Oh yes. Yes! Right. Just stay tame! I'll get it. ...Yes. I'm getting it. Silence!

...Greece, Phraxos, god, deus, ...theo, ...theo dee bump bump ...theo dee bump see ...theodeebumsy ...theodosy! The theodosy problem!

JILLIAN: (Draws breath, about to speak)

MORTON: (Moving right along, not wanting to divert into philosophy.) And his story is so lavish and convincing at a heart level. He makes the reader feel and think even if the reader doesn't know exactly what he is thinking about and even if he doesn't want to think. Just wants to be entertained.

JILLIAN: It is a great book.

MORTON: And the dialog is flawless.

JILLIAN: Yes, it is. It is music. It flows seamlessly.

MORTON: How nice. We enthusiastically agree. Like the lawyers at adjacent urinals when one turns to the other and says, "two legal scholars with the same great idea."

JILLIAN: (Laughs, he smiles) We do indeed. I am so glad. That's why I said Wow. ...And Krauss' book?

MORTON: That's Krauss with two "s"es.

JILLIAN: Yes, I know. Why, *The History of Love*?

MORTON: Why are you so eager to know this?

JILLIAN: Just because. I simply must know what you think about it. To see how our takes line up. Before I die. To see if we are two legal scholars. (Smiles)

MORTON: You mean before I die.

JILLIAN: (Ignoring, repeating) To see how our takes line up. (Impatient, trying to restrain herself, but yielding to it.) I'll go this far first. I feel it's the most courageous piece of fiction I've ever read.

MORTON: You're not going anywhere soon, Jillie.

JILLIAN: Yes, yes, of course. (But her tone trails off to ambiguous, quashing a thought.)

MORTON: Jillian, here's the straight answer. And this is a confession. That novel is so powerful it made me cry! It has. It made me cry. Actually weep. Seriously....

JILLIAN: Oh, I believe you! I know. Me too. Many times.

MORTON: The only time that's ever happened. Even on the second and third readings. When I knew what was going to happen! Unique. Four times! And I've re-read parts of it many other times. The scope and swoop of her imagination! She interleafs so many layers. ...Like your play, by the way.

JILLIAN: (Turns her head aside and holds it there) I'll deserve that someday maybe.

MORTON: But I'm telling you that you do.

JILLIAN: Maybe someday I'll be able to accept it.

MORTON: But you do deserve it. You should accept it now!

JILLIAN: In the near future.

MORTON: In the near future? That's odd. You said the *"near"* future. Why?

JILLIAN: (Head down, mutters) You'll see.

MORTON: Why are you saying this? You're an enigma inside a conundrum today! ...Did you sprinkle a controlled substance on your oatmeal this morning?

JILLIAN: (Smiles, but quickly serious) Please Morton, trust me or I will burst. Let's go a bit further.

MORTON: (Knows that something deep is being communicated, but cannot see through Jillian's smokescreen. Dubious.) Well....

JILLIAN: Thanks. All will become clear shortly. Illuminated. Trust me.

MORTON: If you say so. (Looks at her, suspiciously–fondly, then continues.) She forces the reader to work, and she trusts her reader to do so! Spellbinding. It is what writing should be about. Heartrending, and healing.

JILLIAN: Yes! It is the most gripping novel I've ever read.

MORTON: It reads like Toni Morrison without the mental lactic–acid buildup. (Both laugh)

JILLIAN: Well put. Yes.

MORTON: (Seeming aside) You know, companies have this tool, the Myers–Briggs Indicator that supposedly evaluates personality types or styles.
(Focusing the aside.) It's so–so; but to give you the richest short answer I can give: ...*Ulysses* would be the premiere Intellectual archetype; *The Magus* the premiere Emotional one; and *The History of Love* the exemplar of the Intuitive archetype, if you will.

JILLIAN: I do ...so will. (Both smile at the wordplay and both choose not to pursue it.) I love the book.

MORTON: Why? Now let's talk ground level. Shoptalk me. Why do you love it so much?

JILLIAN: Oh good, Morton! I love when you are energized, when you're feisty!

MORTON: The god you recommend I give obeisance to has smiled upon me, in advance. Take advantage of it. Hurry up, you never know how long feisty will last. ...I never know.

JILLIAN: You go first.

MORTON: No! I'm the elder! (Both laugh at the reference)

JILLIAN: You have re-read it!

MORTON: Of course, Silly. I would not deceive you.

JILLIAN: (Averts her eyes, shamed by his use of that word, but hiding it.) I know that. I was just relishing the fact. Stretching out my enjoyment of the fact.

MORTON: (Undoing the comedy) At least, I'm older than you. (Both laugh again) Go. You start. Beauty before age.

JILLIAN: Well, for starters, it is astonishing how she gets the reader to care about Leo in twenty-three words. Astonishing!

Who's interested in a character that quickly? The first twenty-three words! ...Simply astonishing.

MORTON: (Different tone, simple) I can't think of anyone. (Then waxing to full professorial) Not Dickens. Not Austen. Not Fitzgerald. *No one* else. No one has made me interested in a character that quickly.

Our critiques match. (Resetting the mood) Now, let's be wary of turning this into an, "I love you, I love you more" fest.

JILLIAN: (Laughs) It's too late for that.

MORTON: (Laughs, too) You're good. How'd you get to be so good?

JILLIAN: William and I once played on the word "good," in jive talk, "*baaad*," meaning good.

MORTON: I know. I "dig."

JILLIAN: (Smiles, pleased at his instant shuttling) You tickle me.

MORTON: You and he must have had a beautiful thing going.

JILLIAN: (Acknowledges by gesture) We did.

(Referring back, ignoring his redirection, trusting that Morton will follow.) I know. She's amazing.

(Both sip tea again and a bite of biscotti, more from a need to process what is happening than from hunger.)

JILLIAN: (Long pause, sensing his state) And the ending, there is nothing like it!

MORTON: Oh no! No. We'd better not go there! If we get to talking about the ending, you could work me into a cry again.

JILLIAN: (Smiles tenderly and nods her head, Yes.)

MORTON: (Enunciating each component separately) There is, *nothing*, like it. *Anywhere.*

JILLAN: (Laughing) We wouldn't want that to happen again, would we? Or maybe a cry would be a good thing. Like naughty. And I might join you, and you wouldn't want that to happen.

MORTON: No, we would not.

JILLIAN: That was the royal We?

MORTON: This new god, of whom I'm a devotee, has awakened me. I am entitled to the royal We.

JILLIAN: (Laughs) So be it. It's your turn, ...god's devotee.

MORTON: You really do have a good effect on me, Jillie.

JILLIAN: Thank you, love, but don't dither.

MORTON: "Dither." Great word choice!

JILLIAN: (Rising tone) Morton....

MORTON: I thought you were going to say, "lollygag."

JILLIAN: Might have. Second choice. But lollygagging has too many syllables. Now please.....

MORTON: Here Jillie, this one's for you! Consider it a gift. Because you are so eager. ...I don't know *why*, but you are. I've never experienced you like this. *Did* you sprinkle a controlled substance on your oatmeal this morning? (Quizzical look, slight smile)

JILLIAN: (Laughs, then strains to restrain herself) Morton ... please.

MORTON: By the by, you know that "Gift" in German means poison? Das Gift.

JILLIAN: (Rising tone) Morton....

MORTON: Well then, there is no other way to put this. A lesser account would demean her gift. Krauss —with two "s"es— (he sneaks a glance) has given us one of the most memorable lines in *all* of literature. (Draws breath)

JILLIAN: (Slipping in an interruption, excited. Happy rising voice.) I *know* where you're going, Morton! ...Where Leo says —where she has heroic–pathetic Leo say— "**COULD I BE FAMOUS WITHOUT KNOWING IT?**"

(Both crack up, and keep laughing, in waves. Laughing like stoned college students, heads shaking Yes, Yes, and Yes. Almost crying, about character Leo, and their depth of shared intimacy.)

JILLIAN: (Finally ... through her laughter) One, (laughs again) twenty-three. He, he, he.

MORTON: (Through his laughter) One, (laughs) two, three ...*what*?

JILLIAN: *Page* 123!

MORTON: (Not hearing or not understanding) One, two, three ... what? *Hike*?

(Jillian guffaws! Then Morton guffaws from contagion. When the jag subsides more laughter follows in slower, calmer waves.)

JILLIAN: *One twenty-three!* (Chuckles) That's the *page* number I've commanded myself to memorize! That's where that occurs!

MORTON: (Chuckles) You knock me out!. ...And Leo knocks me out! (More laughing, both heads Yes, Yes, Yes and catching breath.) And Krauss knocks me out. (Rolling laughs again)

JILLIAN: Krauss–with–two–"s"es, (teasing) ...or the other one?

MORTON: Right! Like there could be another one. Thank goodness there isn't! (More laughter at the thought of it)

JILLIAN: Oh, this was good.

MORTON: (After they finally recover enough to talk) I haven't laughed like this in years. I can't remember a time. Oh, thank you. (Starts to laugh again, mildly)

JILLIAN: My pleasure. It's a joy to share this with you.

MORTON: (Aloud, but more to amuse himself) Sour–kraus. (Laughs again)

JILLIAN: (Goes to embrace him. Morton reaches up to hug and hold her, but he accidentally pokes her neck with his pinky finger.) Ooooh!

MORTON: I'm sorry. Are you okay? And I've stubbed my pinky.

JILLIAN: Yes, yes.

(Both take a breath and Jillian drinks some water, stalls....)

JILLIAN: I should be going. I'm going Morton.

MORTON: Go then! I'm ready. (Suppressed laugh, at the reference) Been ready for too long.

JILLIAN: I am, too, Morton. Ready.

Thank you again, for everything. You have meant and mean so much to me. Thank you for letting me become your friend. For the years. For the ...for the ...sharing. (Breaks into tears, then sobs uncontrollably. When she recovers, she blurts out.) For your beautiful mind.

MORTON: You are most welcome. And thank you, for becoming and for being my friend, all these years. For being my soul–daughter. (Wide, open-hearted smile) You are that, you know, Cordelia. (Smiles)

JILLIAN: (Smiles back at the reference, but is caught up again crying.) Oh Morton, thank you. Thank you. Thank you. (Both hug and kiss, on both cheeks) I love you. (Another hug. Both cheeks. Another brief hug.)

(Pause. Pregnant pause. More delay.)

MORTON: (Sensing mood) What is it Jill? Something's up.

JILLIAN: (Choking back a new wave of tears) Morton ...I wrote something. Am writing.

MORTON: What! *What* did you say? No! *What*! (Taps one of his hearing aids twice) Did you say what I think you said?

JILLIAN: Yes. Am writing. I am writing something. Have written.

MORTON: What! How's it coming? After *how* many years? How far along are you?

JILLIAN: Finished! ...Except for the very end.

MORTON: I can't believe it! That's great! What remains? ...When can I read it?

JILLIAN: Tomorrow.

MORTON: *Tomorrow!?*

JILLIAN: We are uttering the final words.

MORTON: *What!* What can *that* mean? *What* did you say? (Long pause) What do you mean!

(Silence. Jillian averts her glance, feeling for his mood.)

MORTON: (Further pause, processing his thoughts and processing her mood.) Wait a minute....

(Another, very long pause) Wait a minute. ...Wait a *mi-nute!*

JILLIAN: (Looks at him with a childlike guilty smile) Uh huh. Uh, huh.

MORTON: (Can't quite believe it. Doesn't know how it's possible.) No! ...Look, Jillian, have mercy. I am old. I must be imagining things. Can I be thinking right? Am I losing it?

JILLIAN: (Unabashed smile) Yes. You are, thinking right.

MORTON: (Rising tone, like a father trying to extract a confession from a child) Jil ...li ...ann?

JILLIAN: Yes.

MORTON: Did you write me into this play or novel, or whatever it is?

JILLIAN: (Broad smile) Yes. (Beaming, then averts eyes) Am.

MORTON: (Mock anger) You *mischievous* imp! Mischievous, naughty, imp!

(Several audible breaths. Understanding continuing to dawn, then smiles, then beaming.) Mischievous, mischievous imp!

JILLIAN: (Sensing his growing understanding, jumps forward) We are uttering them now. We are saying them. *Singing* them, actually. You and me. This is our song. Our swan song.

MORTON: You're having another senior moment! My swan song maybe.

JILLIAN: (Ignoring, returning to the lighthearted mood) I know. I know. But you will like it.

MORTON: You are too much! You are going to give me a heart attack. A heart attack of joy. I love it. And I hate it too. But I love it more.

JILLIAN: You will. It is the best thing I've ever written. Actually. ...

MORTON: (Imitating, to draw her out) Actually ...what?

JILLIAN: (Looks up, now permitting him to see her nakedly, finally confessing, but still not totally.) Actually, the only thing.

MORTON: Now what does *that* mean! You are mystifying me. (Mock playing the pity card) It's not nice to bamboozle old folks. Come on ...'fess up now.

JILLIAN: (Talking honestly but still not yet fully confessing, using one level to mask the other.) It is unique, this, the whole thing. It's like a 3-D sculpture that revolves and twists within the turning. An emotional Calder sculpture, if I may say so.

MORTON: Jillie, what *are* you talking about? You are tantalizing me beyond endurance. I feel that you keep shifting the subject. And purposely! You keep doing it. You are doing it right now! You sly ...fox. Vixen. An imp and a vixen.

(Smiles, mock reprimanding tone again) A naughty, mischievous, vixen imp!

JILLIAN: (Referring back) No, no, Morton! You must endure it! And you must endure, too. You must stay alive to read it. I need to know you will read it. Several times. You'll get it. It requires several readings though, even by a demi-god.

MORTON: I've never heard you so confident. I can't believe it! It's wonderful to hear you like this. (Then reconnecting with the previous thought, playfully.) And how many for ordinary mortals?

JILLIAN: (Purposely reverting to old Modest Self but with awareness and a touch of self-diminishment.) More than several.

MORTON: What a total surprise. What a delightful surprise. ...You fox!

JILLIAN: You'll love it. I know you will. And that will be such a joy to me. ...And a relief.

MORTON: *Relief?* What, "relief?" ...Why a "relief?"

JILLIAN: For *that*, you must read it to find out!

MORTON: I can hardly stand it. I haven't felt like this in years! I am intrigued, and you are a fox.

JILLIAN: Assure me you will read it.

MORTON: You know I will. I assure you. First thing.
(Pause, talking to himself but aloud for her benefit)
Overly–modest–you boldly assert that I will love it? I love that!

JILLIAN: I say so! (Pause) It *is* like nothing else. ...Except for Krauss.

MORTON: Krauss again! (Pausing for breath) This whole conversation is an emotional Calder! A Calder–Krauss.
(Pensive moment, then smiles) A Linden-Calder-Krauss. That has a nice ring to it by the way.

JILLIAN: (Undistracted, referring back, driving her purpose) But some things, like a Calder–Krauss, require complexity. Even so, they must be delivered simply.

MORTON: (Fishing, hoping for focus) Like what, for example?

JILLIAN: (Ignoring) You know who taught me that?

MORTON: Who?

JILLIAN: Ms. "Krauss–with–two–"s"–es."

MORTON: (Frustrated, but genuinely intrigued and tickled) You are revealing and still concealing at the same time.

JILLIAN: Language can do that, you know.

MORTON: Yes, I am aware of that.

JILLIAN: And, you know who taught me *that*?

MORTON: I'll bite ...Who?

JILLIAN: *You*!

MORTON: No!

JILLIAN: And, how to do it!

MORTON: No!

JILLIAN: Especially in drama.

MORTON: No! (Pretended regret) I wish I hadn't taught you so much.

JILLIAN: (Returning to point) I will finish it right away. As soon as I get home. This afternoon. I'll mail it to you immediately, next day delivery, or I can hand deliver it. I'll send it. Please read it. Tell me you will. Right away. The first reading.

MORTON: That soon! Are you kidding me? (Almost to himself) So you've dipped your toes in the water again? He, he, he. This is a wonderful surprise!

JILLIAN: Good. I think it will delight you.

MORTON: Is *that* why you asked me if I can still read? ...That *is* why you asked me if I can still read!

JILLIAN: It is. Yes. It is.

MORTON: You sly, mischievous vixen!

JILLIAN: Please say no more. Let me guide you in this. The Linden-Calder-Krauss is still in spin.

Morton: Now who is being feisty!

JILLIAN: I should go.

MORTON: Oh, I loved this. You have sprinkled sunshine into an otherwise dull and dreary life, and made it sparkle.

JILLIAN: I will go now.

MORTON: Go! The afternoon is upon us.
(Jillian weeping, bends and kisses Morton again, then breaks away, exits hurriedly without looking back.)

MORTON: (Talking mostly to himself) I can't wait to get it.

Reprise [3c]

So, before it gets too late, before memory, body or will sputter unreliably and then disconnect irrevocably, I bequeath this to you, and to Nicolette.

There is no perchance. There is no afterdream. *I* will decide, not entropy! While I have mind enough to remember, body enough to do, and will enough to command them, I will act.

You wanted to know me, intimately, most intimately. *Eccomi qua.* Here I am. My innermost self, my real self. William and Morton started my mind, and William gave me my sexuality. Actually, he, William that is, did more than that. He synced my mind and my sexuality. The result: my voice. You'll see. You'll hear. You *are* hearing it. It is speaking right now. It is *singing* right now. A *celestial* voice, if I may say so.

Tomorrow, Morton, you will receive a signed copy of these documents, my *Confession* and William's *Walrus*, and some legal stuff. It will illuminate the whole truth and nothing but the truth. Perhaps this will be the final thing you read. Beam up your lamp and magnifier. It must be read slowly. That's why I said cryptically that, "slow is good, sometimes." I pretended I was making a joke. A weak joke. But I knew. I knew that circumstances force "slow" upon you. Enjoy it. I believe you will.

I hope you understand and forgive me. For both. Perhaps you sense what I mean, although I think not, and really hope not. Not yet. Not just yet. You will very shortly know exactly what I mean. All will be revealed. Please forgive me and embrace me. I want to feel your embrace for this. Actually, I do. I know you will love it. I can feel your love and pride beaming through the ether to me. So this, Morton, this this, is my amend to you and it is also my bequest to Nicolette. I want you to know that I now feel fully absolved and content.

Bucket list:

1. Bring myself to the farthest reaches of what William had awakened and begun to develop in me.

2. Atone to Morton and give to him something he will enjoy, relish,

even cherish, and which may even invigorate him and keep him alive.

3. Honor the three greatest artists of my time who have so enriched my life: Pink Floyd, John Fowles, and Nicole Krauss. I am at peace, all the way around. I am content.

(I'd like to address you in particular, Nicole. Thank you for your book and thanks for your courage to experiment the way you did. Your book *is* like nothing else, anywhere. Morton and I agreed about that, so that settles the matter. I hope you are intensely proud of it. And, if this story–play–story is seven–tenths of that book, I am happy. Thank you.)

4. Fourth, but primary: raise Nicolette to be a real human being: loving, caring, rounded, independent, having her own voice, and capable of earning her own living.

Nicolette, I love you so much and want you to know how much joy you have brought me. Immeasurable. Look upon this bequest as an act of love and courage. I will not devolve piecemeal into that Good Night. I will not saddle you with what promises to become a joyless and bruising descent. Remember me as I have been, and as we were. Remember our good times and the love we shared. And your father, too. He would have loved you very much and been so proud of you.

And simply tell little William and little Roberta that Grandma died. Tell them that little bugs live for a short time, and that people, like Grandma, live for a much longer time, but that even trees, like the ones they see outside, don't live forever. When the old trees fall down, they make room for little trees to grow up. Be direct with them, Nicolette, please; they will accept it and will adapt well. Take my word for it.

I smile at all of you. And a big, long hug to all of you.

[**Advance Directive**: To any director who wishes to produce this play/screenplay/story, you must coordinate the last syllable, below, with ending of the 12':24" version of, "*A Saucerful of Secrets*," on Pink Floyd's, "*Ummagumma*." The volume should be soft for the first eight minutes approximately, the mysterious music just barely audible. Then, at around 10':30" the volume should continuously slowly rise with the soaring ending. That ending, *Celestial Voices*, like the *Chorale* of *Beethoven's Ninth*, should augment, compete

and finally coalesce with Jillian's speaking part, that is to say, this,

3c. Nevertheless, my voice, Jillian's voice, should be distinct,

prevailing over the music 2:1.]

I am en route now to the post office, and from there heading

up to Mount Washington, New Hampshire, the windiest place in

the United States. There, where gale force winds are common, I

may be swept off. There, if the force is with me, I shall dive as

elegantly as possible, and my last word shall be,

Saucerfulllllllll.

Part 4

Epilog

Hi, it's me again. Nicolette. What follows is one of only two other extant pieces of Jillian's writing. It was in her drawer along with the outtake —her dialog with Morton about the title— that I worked into the *Preface* earlier. The other material was in a sealed manila envelope with the words, "This too, not until thirty," clearly printed on it. It was obviously for me.

A spirit of confidence and joy pervades the writing. It is, from quite an unexpected angle, an X-ray of William's *Walrus*, and her *Confession*. I include it here because, first of all, it shows her growth into further maturity from the extended–release nourishment she got from the three other *Walrus* characters, and secondly, to show her being exuberant and non-modest. Even a little show-offy. It shows Mom at play, playing about and with the plays.

It shall be her epitaph.

[Jillian's] *Journal*

Just for fun.

This will be conducted like a catechism in the hyper-naturalistic style of James Joyce's *Ulysses* in the section where Leopold Bloom is interrogated.

First children, let's play "Archaeologist." Like using Ground-Penetrating radar (GPr) to locate, unearth, and establish the provenance of undetected treasures, we will use our Acoustical/Prosody Recognition radar (APRr) to reveal unsuspected harmonics from *Hamlet* that lie scattered under the sand and sandstorm of words that swirl above and throughout, *The Walrus* and *My Confession*. Lines from *Hamlet* are preceded by a star, thus *.

1.   a- *The Walrus*

        I am tame, sir. Pronounce. {H: ACT III, Scene 2, line 302}

        WILLIAM: (to Jillian) "I am tame." (ACT IV, Scene 4)

Now cracks a noble heart. {*H*: (Horatio) ACT V, Scene 2, line 364}

HALEY: "All our hearts crack as one." (*H*: ACT V, Scene 2)

b- *The Confession, Introduction*, 3a

Call me what instrument you will, though you fret me, you cannot play upon me. {*H*: ACT III, Scene 2, lines 361-363}

JILLIAN: "You cannot know what exactly what was fiction and what fact, so intuit what you will, that blend is yours."

Do you see yonder cloud that's almost in shape of a camel?
By th' mass and 'tis--like a camel indeed.
Methinks it is like a weasel.
It is backed like a weasel.
Or like a whale.
Very like a whale. {*H*: (Hamlet / Polonius) Act III, Scene 3, lines 367-373}

JILLIAN: "Yes I had a hand in it, but only the tiniest part. More like a finger, more like a fingernail, more like a clipping from the pinky of the non-dominant hand."

c- *My Confession:*

I am tame, sir. Pronounce. {*H*: ACT III, Scene 2, line 302}

JILLIAN: (to Morton) "I am tame, sir. Pronounce."

*The lady doth protest too much, methinks. {H: ACT III, Scene 2, line 225}

MORTON: "Methinks you fish for something."

*To be, or not to be, that is the question: {H: ACT III, Scene 1, line 56}

MORTON: "This god ...does he intervene? That is the question."

*The slings and arrows of outrageous fortune.... {H: ACT III, Scene 1, line 58}

JILLIAN: "the slings and arrows that outrage [your body]"

*It is as easy as lying. Govern these ventages ... {H: ACT III, Scene 2, line 348}

JILLIAN: "Simply govern these ventages ..." (again, similar rhythm) "Simply give obeisance to..."

[By prosody or rhythm, (reversed sentence construction)]

*Madness in great ones must not unwatched go. {H: ACT III, Scene 2, line 190}, [and]

My words fly up, my thoughts remain below. Words without thoughts never to heaven go. {H: ACT III, Scene 3, lines 97-98}

MORTON (to JILLIAN) "Two codgers confused at the same time makes not for coherent conversation."

Readiness is all. {H: ACT V, Scene 2, line 218}

MORTON (to JILLIAN) "Go, then. I am ready. Been ready for too long."

JILLIAN (to MORTON) "I am too, Morton. Ready."

d- *The Confession, Reprise,* 3c

To sleep, perchance to dream--ay, there's the rub {H: ACT III, Scene,1, line 65}

JILLIAN "There is no perchance. There is no afterdream."

2. What numbers and numerical adjectives, in ascending order, appear in William's play and Jillian's story-play-story? Do not repeat duplicates. If and only if relevant, supply correlatives.

In *The Walrus*:

One (inch, more, dance), first, two, halfway, both, twice (per year), few, three, 3 (o'clock), 4 (years older, -day weekend, couples, -decades remove, decades ago), 5 (dances, -minute span), six (sigma, years old, bridesmaids) 7(PM, full days), nine (years old), 10 (minutes), ten, 17th (Street), eighteen ("dates" / "sessions"), [West] 23d (Street), thirty-six (years), '50s, '60's, eighty (when I'm [age]), one hundred (percent certainty, percent healed), 300 (times thought about [sexually]), one thousand (days).

In _The Confession, Introduction_ [3a]:

three (decades).

In _My Confession [3b]_:

one, first, once, two, 2, second, a few, 3, 3-D, third, several, four (times wept), many, ten, twenty, forty, forty-three, fifty, one hundred, 123 (page), 159 (page), 1667, 1905.

In _The Confession, Reprise [3c]_:

• 1, 2, 3, 4, fourth, 2:1 (ratio), 10':30" (minutes: seconds), 12':24" (minutes: seconds)

3. What animals are mentioned in the play and the story-play-story? Itemize separately and in order.

In _The Walrus_:

• dog, kitten, cat (Siamese), elephant, squirrel, possum, blue jays, monkeys.

In *My Confession*:

- fox, vixen.

4. What foods are mentioned? In order.

In *The Walrus*:

- Thai, Chinese, paella, scones, apple turnover, Indian, broccoli naan, salad, eggplant parm.

In *The Confession*:

- tarte, biscotti.

5.What beverages are mentioned?

In *The Walrus*:

- an unspecified drink in a bar, beer, a cordial, cappuccino, wine, iced tea with lemon, gin and tonic, tea, coffee, Sauvignon blanc, Chianti, flavored brandy liqueur.

In *My Confession*:

- a cup of tea

6. What other noteworthy key words or key lines occur in different contexts throughout *The Bequest*? Itemize where, if relevant.

In *The Walrus*:

magnificent/ly,

[JILLIAN to WILLIAM] "That *stupid* play or screenplay, whatever it is."

In *My Confession:*

[MORTON to JILLIAN] "...this play or novel, or whatever it is."

--------------Break off here?

7.   *My Other Confession*

We had one or two dates, both of which were nice, Chinese restaurant level nice. He was older by one year. In high school I had witnessed several loving relationships and I wanted one desperately. I wanted the chance for a real and loving relationship. Everybody seemed to like him too. He asked me to the Christmas Dance, which was a formal occasion. I was happy to accept and bought a new dress for the dance.

Background: His previous was prettier than me. I was cute but she was gorgeous. I knew that I was second fiddle, definitely.

She exuded and flaunted sex. One day he and she had an argument right outside school, about her attire. He wanted her not to allow others to see what he wished her to save for his eyes alone. I liked that. I assumed that that's how he would be with me. I idealized him for that concern. What everyone in my grade knew and what he did not know, was that at every classroom change, she, with utter nonchalance, provided an even more spectacularly provocative momentary display. Not one off, routinely! For us girls it was pretty upsetting and intense. I can only imagine its impact on the guys! Those afternoons must have been Semen City. They were all crazy for her.

We all knew that she and he had been sexually active. She broke up with him after some months. In my mind she was my competition.

The day before the dance he told me he wouldn't be able to take me to it, that he had to work, that it wasn't practical to go because by the time he got home and then took me there it would be almost over, but he still wanted to see me that night. I was so saddened and confused. I didn't know what to do. I had the sinking feeling too that he would *never* have done this to her. So the idea shot through me that he didn't like me as much as her, or as much as I liked him. Or that maybe he didn't want to show me off as his date. But ...he said that he wanted to see me that night.

I didn't want to tell my family the truth because I didn't want them to be angry with him. I couldn't go to the dance by myself because everyone else was going as couples. I made up a story to my parents about how I would get to the dance, lying, which I had almost never done before, I felt so guilty. While I dressed for the dance Mom was helping me with my hair and my sister was helping me with my make-up. They took a photo of me and were so excited for me. I felt like crying but I had to keep up the front. The photo they took shows me smiling as if everything were all right. Now I look at that photo and realize that that night my childhood ended.

I can't remember how I got to his house. My mind was such a blur. I felt so guilty that I can't remember exactly, even today. Dad must have driven me. But the whole way over my gut kept telling me, 'this is all wrong.' I didn't even want to leave the car. I felt so let down and sad. I also felt guilty because everybody trusted me so much. I was so trustworthy. I never lied. And they were so excited for me. I felt like a disappointment to them and to myself.

First of all, he was dressed okay, in jeans and a shirt, but he had not changed into anything nice to complement my outfit. I felt foolish and embarrassed. Here I was in a really nice dress and he was in work clothes. He ushered me down to the basement. I remember it was cold down there. Very cold. There were a lot of trophies around and a pool table. The whole scene felt like a dungeon. There was no comfortable seating. It was really cold, I was shaking from the cold and from feeling scared and uncomfortable. I walked around a little bit, looking at trophies, trying to get a little comfortable, but really, it felt like two boxers in a ring eyeing each other up. I wanted to run.

The room was dark. He came over to me and kissed me. Then fondled my breasts. No words of romance. Next, he started unbuttoning the buttons in back. As he was trying to take down the front of my dress my necklace caught. It broke and fell to the floor. This felt all wrong. I had imagined a more romantic setting and that all this would have started not from a lie. And with some love.

I didn't have the voice to say No. I felt trapped. He was my ride home. It was too far to walk. I had put trust in him because I had seen him be considerate and protective towards his previous. I was shocked feeling my top coming down. I had never been even partly naked in front of a guy before. I tried to get over the shock of it. I told myself that if I want to have a romantic relationship these things happen. He took my hand to his cock, which was hard, and he opened his belt and started taking down his pants. He pulled down his pants and took my hand again to his naked cock, to jerk him off.

I vaguely remember the two of us laying on some hard cold surface. He pushed my head down to his cock. I had heard some girls talk about that, blowing a guy, but I didn't know what you do. I was scared. I hated being in this position, it was so rushed, I felt more like a whore than a girlfriend. I had the thought, 'just get it over with,' but I didn't know what "it" was. I was frightened. I was awkward. I didn't know what I was supposed to do. And I had no desire to do it. I felt on his part no special desire for me. We weren't even officially boyfriend and girlfriend yet. Who was I to him? This was expected? Right away? Did she? Second fiddle.

Whether we were on the floor or I was kneeling I don't really remember. I don't want to. I remember It was cold and I was shaking. I was overwhelmed. I thought, This can't be right, He didn't do anything to prepare me, no romantic buildup. My tumble of thoughts rolled on, Maybe this is what girls do, some girls. And, What if he comes in my mouth, What am I supposed to do with it? Do they to spit it out? I don't have a tissue. Do they drink it? Am I supposed to? And, What if I don't do it right?

I didn't know when he was about to come. He shot, and part of it went in my eye and part on the cuff of my sleeve. It burned in my eye. He was unaware of my distress or unconcerned about it.

A few days later my mother asked me what that stain was on my dress. I told her it was orange juice that I had at the dance.

What *could* I have said?

I hadn't cleaned it off at home because I wanted my mom to figure it out and magically save me. She took me at my word.

He eventually took me home which I also don't remember. He didn't smile at me tenderly or treat me with any heartfelt endearment, or hug me or thank me, let alone kiss me.

I had to lie to everybody all over again about what the dance was like, about what a nice evening I had. I wished none of it had ever happened, had been saved from it all. I was troubled and ashamed about what had happened. And the way it happened. The whole experience felt wrong.

I had trusted that he would guide me into a physical relationship with the same care and respect I had witnessed. I wanted a loving experience so much that I convinced myself that if I gave him everything he wanted, he would grow to love me.

Long story short, ...three years later I realized that this was going nowhere, and even if it did, I would be continuously unsatisfied, soulwise. Culturally and intellectually, too. And especially, physically. I won't go into that. At the end, he cried. He had come to appreciate and, up to his capacity, love me. But there was so much missing. I could no longer ignore it. I knew it was all wrong. I had cried it all out, for months, before. I closed that door and never looked back.

For the following decade I trudged across an unending romantic-sexual desert, interspersed with a few withered oases plus one real oasis. But then the world changed. It suddenly became lush and varied, with mountains, rivers, fields and seacoasts, with trees of all sorts from Podocarpus Gracilior to Sequoia Sempervirens, with all sorts of fauna from cougar, bear, and red-brown squirrel to flocks of birds! I met William.

He overwrote everything. Anything previous evaporated, was expunged. He helped me to realize that —as he put it— I was worth much more than I had ever let myself even *imagine*. About that first relationship, which I had to remember in increasing detail at his insistence —which was painful for both of us, and absolutely necessary for me to get free of it— he said in his "put-it-in-a-nutshell" way, that anything multiplied by zero or nearly zero, is zero, or nearly zero. My first was incapable of connecting deeply nor interested in trying to, no matter how full my loving and giving had been. I had only pieces of a Self then. I had tried to overlook it but there was an unbridgeable rent in the fabric of our soul relationship. I regret that I didn't realize it sooner.

I am so lucky that someone came along who wanted to know me and grow me as deeply and fully as William did. He thrilled to grow me. It wasn't easy. I had to trust him totally. But he earned it and proved out. His love for me, and lust, were always at high pitch. I knew he wanted the best for me and for me to be my best.

We were such an unlikely a couple. He named us, as if we were the lead characters of a Disney movie, "The Improbables." This was our inside joke. I was blessed.

I grew him too. He said so. I knew it too, gradually, eventually. But our whole journey would not have started if he hadn't given to me and demanded of me the way he did. He risked everything to ignite us.

Part 5

Preamble to *Professor Seiden's Last Seminar*

Hi. Yes, it's me, Nicolette, again. Morton also bequeathed to me these transcripts of his last Creative Writing Seminar. We rehearsed them once although he didn't need to practice; his grasp of the material and his style of exposition was still flawless. He did it to allow us to go down Memory Lane, to reminisce about Mom, and her and his remembrances of Father. He did it even more so, I'm sure, to encourage me to keep the faith, to become a writer. He approved a draft of this introduction and I also audited his classes. He was spellbinding. His health was also failing.

Professor Seiden's Last Seminar (PSLS)

Lecture 1: Introduction and Definitions

Good afternoon.

Shortly after conception parts of us are shaved away, discarded, and we are thereby shaped into species-specific and unique beings. Apoptosis. Sometime after that we also begin a correlated descent, asymmetric and usually slow, back to the inorganic realm. Organismic apoptosis. My "discard date" is imminent; yours is not; probably. So, do not waste time.

The department cajoled me back, "by popular demand" so they told me, for a last hurrah, an emeritus encore, a swan song. They either thought I had nothing better to do with my time or they thought it would be therapeutic for me. Both, probably. Also, my assistant, Nicolette Linden, probably had a hand in it. So the school broke precedent. *Eccomi qua.* So, here I am.

I will teach directly when I can and when I cannot Nicolette will fill in for me. The department has cleared this, so you will get full credit. My office hours are posted, but uncertain due to health concerns and my waning energy level. Call first, both of us. You have our numbers. You will most likely not get a second or third chance to interact with me on a one-on-one basis as you normally would, so use what I offer you immediately. We will study some of the best literary creations that exist. I will teach you to recognize techniques that the authors used to form vibrant literary works. Utilize these methods and ideas in your work. Make them your own. Embody them in your work. Nicolette will critique your writing drafts and the few tiny homework assignments I will give you.

I will lecture on the following novels. Among the non-starred items you will pick three more to read:

Mark Twain, *Tom Sawyer* 2 and *Huckleberry Finn* 1
Joseph Conrad, *Lord Jim* 2
Theodore Dreiser, *An American Tragedy* 2
F. Scott Fitzgerald, *The Great Gatsby* 3
James Joyce, *Ulysses* 5 [* required]
D. H. Lawrence, *Lady Chatterley's Lover* 2
Anthony Burgess, *A Clockwork Orange* 2
John Fowles, *The Magus* 5 [* required]
Tim O'Brien, *The Things They Carried* 3
Nicole Krauss, *The History of Love* 4 [* required]

Nicolette Linden, *The Bequest* 7 (* which you've read over intersession in the run-up to this course.)

The Department gave me *carte blanche,* and I will use it. This class will combine both textual exposition and creative writing technique. You will learn more in this semester than two summers at the Iowa Writers Workshop. That is quite a claim, but you'll see. We will proceed from the most contemporary texts back to the most foundational. The reason for this is that you can always obtain critiques other than mine on the earlier works, in case....

To begin.... In my opinion, and it is generally agreed, that the Parthenon is the most beautiful building of the ancient Western world; of the Medieval world, Notre Dame Cathedral; and of the modern world, the Eiffel Tower. The Tower, whichever way we view it, feels light and airy and lifts up our spirits, yet it is composed of solid steel. Linden's *Bequest* can, and should, be visualized as a literary equivalent of the Eiffel Tower because each perspective implicates something essential about the overall three dimensional architecture. Each side —Nicolette's, William's, Jillian's and Morton's— is equally important. I will analyze the structural components of this four-sided edifice so that, as student-writers, you understand how the architect created it.

Definition: *Literature*; a written work that molds its constituent parts into a unity, a unity that furthers our imaginative perception and is sometimes a landmark in the arc of literary development. Please note that I did not say, "a good read," or, "a best seller." For a book to be evaluated as belonging to the canon of great books, it must have a beautiful flow, must be passionately appreciated by its readers and, once in a while, may break new literary ground. *The Bequest* qualifies in all respects. It certainly breaks new ground.

Now, with all of the homages contained within *The Bequest,* you undoubtedly suspect that these lectures too are an homage, and indeed they are: a two-way homage: Nicolette's to me for being her parents' cherished literature instructor and more importantly, mine to Nicolette because I find her work worthy of inclusion on my reading list. Your suspicion is herewith confirmed. That much is perhaps obvious. But hidden in this choreographed verbal ballet there is yet another homage that I bet you would not have detected: mine to Jillian. I am honoring her private wish given voice by Nicolette in the middle of her *Preface*:

She [Jillian] said —more like admitted— that she wanted a loving reader to feel and, hopefully, to recognize every stitch of her artistic needlework. But, if not, they should at least enjoy a rollercoaster ride of a read.

So then, I am also fulfilling Jillian's wish embedded within the wider context of her daughter's novel. I'm also certain that this quote is a foil for Nicolette herself, for her wish, unstated. *Every* stitch we haven't time to detail, but I will expose and detail the most salient ones. So, here's to you, Jillian, and William, and even more so to you, Nicolette, for breaking new ground!

Your *rapt* attention is required from here on because *The Bequest* reads so fast and my analysis will likewise be speedy. Fasten your seatbelts, raptors.

To understand *The Bequest* as–a–whole it is imperative that you understand its **framing arc**. Without understanding that, you can neither truly understand the novel structurally nor how

Nicolette integrated its parts into a whole, molded its parts into a unity. The frame is **sine qua non**. Without it, there is no novel.

...Let's get to work unpacking this treasure.

Foreshadowing, induction, recursion, intertext, and sometimes *metatext*, are five concepts that I will illustrate straightaway with the text. Above and beyond these though, the most important element of literary creativity cannot be taught. It is *Imagination*; the central organizing principle of any work; the mind using these five concepts as well as others. I will spotlight these concepts and how certain writers used them but, most importantly, I will show how they dared exercise *Imagination*. They risked going where others had not gone before.

Definition: *Induction*: the writer's purposeful statement *or* purposeful omission of overt statement that is designed to bring about a desired reaction in the reader-audience. To do this, the writer projectively-identifies with the reader or audience, meaning, they know how they would feel if this scene were unfolding in front of them. A perfect illustration of this occurs at the end of *Walrus*

Act II, Scene 3. Jillian's response to William's question whether she would like to meet Roberta and Caitlin, characters three and four, is, "No! I don't know. No." Caitlin opens Act II Scene 4 asking her sister, "So, when are William and Jillian supposed to be here?" All the myriad back-and-forth changes in Jillian's mind are imagined by the reader–audience! The volumes of debate that Jillian must have gone through are supplied by the reader. Nothing is stated. Her motivation is dramatized through action and dialog. In the end, her curiosity has won out. The playwright did not have to enumerate her reasons and rebuttals. We imagine them. Jillian's debate was *induced* in the reader's mind, subconsciously.

And there are many, many other instances of induction. William was a master of this technique; refer, for instance, to the bicycle bell moment in *Walrus* Act III Scene 1. Jillian learned this from him; refer to the many moments in *My Confession,* where she induces *my* inquiry, such as, "You know who taught me that?" which she teasingly repeated a few lines later, "And, you know who taught me *that*?" to which I responded with, "I'll bite ...Who?"

I've changed my mind! I will backpedal here and illustrate *Imagination*. Let's start with the Granddaddy of Western Literature, the crown jewel. I ask you, What is *Hamlet* about?

Yes, yes. ...Of course. But besides each of your answers, I propose that it is about, *Imagination.* Listen up. The *Ur*-Hamlet material existed. We believe that Shakespeare noodled on it in 1593. He must have asked himself: How can I bring this material to life? His answer —in 1600— was to write a play about a character who doesn't want to be in the position, and hence the play, he is in! He starts as a zero point. Keep this keenly and foremost in mind, because it figures crucially in my critique of Linden's work.

To reiterate, Shakespeare brought Hamlet to life by making him doubly-conscious; that is, he is like an objective scientist needing proof of a preposterous assertion —the ghost— and then worse, the conclusion he must draw from events and then choose to act or not act on that evidence. He is also a deeply feeling person. He is both with himself and monitoring himself from a director's view; mindfulness personified. Double consciousness, or, as I prefer to call it, Awareness. He is Shakespeare under a mask. *Hamlet*: "The play's the thing wherein I'll catch the conscience of the king." A play within a play. *The Walrus*: Theater of the Mind within ordinary theater. *The Bequest*: narrative containing dramas within narrative.

In *Hamlet* we do not get an ordinary character with an agenda; instead, the invented character is aware of himself on the picture–plane of his lifespace while simultaneously viewing himself from a director's chair, directing himself the character, and even, sometimes, confiding his thoughts to the audience! This confiding is also a form of *metatextuality*. Much more about that term, presently.

With that as preface, let's turn to Nicolette Linden's, *The Bequest*. This work is like nothing else in literature. If it resembles *anything* structurally other than the Eiffel Tower, it resembles most Picasso's, *Les Demoiselles D'Avignon,* and like that painting it requires continuous perspective shifting to be enjoyed and appreciated. *The Bequest* is narrative embracing drama, embracing several dramas in fact. It reads like an almost-living

Rubik's cube of perspectives. Four perspectives: Nicolette's, William's, Jillian's and mine, Morton's.

<u>Definition</u>: *Recursion*; something read presently harks back to something read earlier; we sense that something else is going on, perhaps many other things, and this produces a depth and richness we feel even if we can't quite label it. We work to understand it: the under-harmonics amplify the earlier-felt something. This is how "a truly great story teaches its readers how to read it." Multiple recursions. You need examples? I'll use what Jillian had provided in her Introduction to *The Confession.* There she reminds us how often the words, "red," "blood," and "bloody" re-occur —recur— in another of Shakespeare's masterpieces, *Macbeth*. Repeated words develop a theme or mood.

Nicolette had to find a way to both present and integrate four viewpoints, each one being convincing in its own right. Here is her blueprint:

Part 1, *The Preface* introduces, then subsumes,

Part 2, *The Walrus,* William's five-act play. She then switches perspective to

Part 3, Jillian's, *The Confession*, which contains Jillian's play, *My Confession*, 3b, itself a *tour de force* of dramatic writing.

Part 4, the *Epilog,* starts with Nicolette's miniscule introduction and promptly gives way to Jillian's *Journal.* Finally, she gives us

Part 5, *Professor Seiden's Last Seminar,* (*PSLS*), an outsider's perspective on the foregoing four parts. Recursion and metatext woven into brocade.

This disquisition is, therefore, inescapably metatextual. Definition: *Metatext*; A character or narrator who exists on two planes simultaneously: *text and metatext*. For example, right now, because I am your teacher, you are hearing me live, in the present. Obviously. Text. But others will be reading this. For them, my primary role is as a character, and secondarily as a teacher. I am also their teacher, but in a different sense. Metatext.

With the insertion of these lectures as Part 5, the character interacting with Jillian in the *My Confession* dialog, Morton Seiden, becomes a major actor in the overall structure of *The Bequest*. We have here a rare instance of mirroring by technique, one that Jillian had used in her *Confession*. There, Jillian had captured our — Jillian's and my— dialog within her *Confession*. Nicolette is having a literary "conversation" with Jillian. This is *Intertext*, which I will define shortly.

Also additionally, and I hope by now obvious, Nicolette's mirroring of text as both metatext and intertext will, in a future moment, be *recursion*; and that moment is *now*. Let me make this perfectly clear: Jillian's technique was authentically her own in Part 3, *The Confession*. But now —as we retrospectively view the novel as-a-whole— we can see that Nicolette introduced Morton the character early on in the *Prolog* and in the *Morton and Jillian Discuss the Title* dialog. There he is part of the text. Here and now, he is both the textual instructor in front of you and the metatextual figure who is also deconstructing Nicolette's novel for readers.

Furthermore, the incorporated M and J dialog serves as foreshadowing. Her *Preface*, don't forget, was written years after Jillian's *Confession*. As writers, you must grapple to link the spacetime coordinates, but as casual readers you can merely enjoy the book ferociously. As writers however, you must visualize a book's bones and joints. When she insinuated my lectures into *The Bequest,* Nicolette knew this would let me provide you with a literary anatomy class. So clever. So beautiful, too.

To return. At one stroke, all parts of the orchestra come together; metatext, intertext, foreshadowing and recursion are melded in a flow so smooth that it is unnoticed by most readers; but not unfelt. Even an alert reader could not have known this —the spacetime coordinates— until much later in the book if they reflected on the flow at all. But you, as future writers, are now cognizant and conscious of them. Are we doubly-conscious yet?

As I said earlier, it is absolutely imperative that you understand the **framing arc** of *The Bequest* as–a–whole. The frame is ***sine qua non***. I repeat, without it, there is no novel. Re-fasten your seatbelts.

My exposition of *The Bequest* contains many recursions —
there is simply no way around it. It is inescapable due to the
multiplexity of Nicolette's imagination. Added to that, there are
many moments of intertextual play, both internally, meaning, *within*
the separate parts of *The Bequest*, and externally, meaning, with
reference to *outside* texts. <u>Definition</u>: *intertext;* is a dialog between
a current text and a previous work. The intertext dialog may also
be covert or overt. I will illustrate this wrinkle momentarily. You
must understand *The Bequest's* coordinates. You, as ordinary
readers, must work to grasp it in your own way —think Derrida—
but as aspiring writers, you must apprehend its architecture, its
groundplan. This requires much *more* work —therefore these
lectures— but because Nicolette's text is so brilliantly conceived it
should be a labor of love.

The Bequest flows very fast, very often. It is dense and
recursive; it is a literary Rubik's *sphere*. I could justify an argument
that besides being a novel, which is narrative —in this case
interwoven with drama— that all three, *The Bequest* as-a-whole,
The Walrus, and Jillian's *Confession* exhibit what Nabokov has

called the exquisite 'precision of poetry.' Great phrase. <u>Definition</u>: a prose poem; is a piece of writing having obvious poetic qualities including intensity and density, with prominent rhythms and images, and with distinctive and repetitive diction.

"*Intensity*" and "*density,*" and the other definitional facets? ...If you don't think that *The Walrus, The Confession* and *The Bequest* as-a-whole qualify under that definition —especially *The Walrus*— then I don't know what does. Moreover, if you will be kind enough to cite for me one work of literature that *does* qualify whereas these three do *not*, you will earn my gratitude, an A+ for this course, and a most enthusiastic letter of recommendation!

This course, *PSLS,* spotlights various literary techniques for a class of advanced student writers. You. You all. *Tutti voi.* Right now, as I am sincerely speaking to you —*this* utterance— is a metatextual device of Nicolette's! If you are hearing this live, you are a student in my class. If you are reading *PSLS*, then I am in your mind teaching you, but you hear my words in your own voice. Nicolette captured my lectures and she incorporated them into the metafictional panorama that I am unpacking for you. Ingenious.

(Think Baudrillard: the distinction between reality and representation, or better in this case, their *interpenetration*.)

What is gained by this double reality? What advantage does it serve? By weaving this brocade, Nicolette created a flexible mechanism that permits her intimacy with both me and the reader, while providing her with authorial distance to place her strategic interventions. This is how she anchored and buttressed the component pieces of *The Bequest* into a whole! How like the Eiffel Tower. And how like *Les Demoiselles!* ...More about this momentarily.

----Let's take a half-minute break for a stretch. My back really needs it.----

Okay. There are seven levels of Imagination and Intention operating right now. My intention is to teach you:

1) how to recognize techniques that some talented writers have used to make their texts vivid and coherent;

2) how to read and deconstruct text generally;

3) how Nicolette's all-important framing narrative allowed her to introduce her father's play, *The Walrus* and;

4) her mother's work, *The Confession,* as well as Jillian's *Journal*;

5) how Nicolette subtly mirrors her mother's metatextual device by incorporating me into the story. ...To remind you, in Jillian's play I was an unwitting accomplice; in this, Nicolette's novel, I knew what she was doing and, frankly, marveled at it.

6) how Nicolette utilized these lectures to provide a literary anatomy lesson. By absorbing *PSLS* into her work she allows me to show you how to dissect a multilayered novel and how to deconstruct or even reverse engineer a complex work of literature, and;

7) most importantly, how all three writers set a *very* high bar of *Imagination* to vault.

There may be another level to Nicolette's recursive metafiction but that is a speculation I will save for a later lecture.

You have a *living* example of metafiction if you realize that Professor Seiden is not just a character who has the same name as me, but *is* me. Think Borges, only much less heady! I will have much more to say about the one-off fact of my being co-opted into *both* Jillian's play and Nicolette's novel in upcoming lectures. Hold this in mind.

The beating heart of the work as–a–whole is Part 2, *The Walrus.* It is the ignition and the engine. It sparked in counterpoint Jillian's play, *My Confession,* which was written many years later. Years still later, Jillian's daughter, Nicolette —their daughter— determined that they must be published. The world needed to read them. And she needed to honor her parents by finding some way to bring those documents "into the light." To accomplish this, she had to 1) quit her job and 2), as writer, devise a narrative arc that integrated the two major components, the works of her mother and her father. I am stressing this as foundational because those two works are so different in voice and format: her father's, pure drama; and her mother's, a panini of narrative and drama. It was *essential* that the author find her own voice within whatever framework she eventually created.

So, here's how she did it. She imagined herself to a near zero point as the intermittent narrator of the overall work! Okay, lots of writers have done that, from Chaucer on. But *she* so consistently underplays her own importance to the work that one has to jog one's memory —more like slap one's mind!— to recall that she is the artist who integrated the parts into a whole. Her influence is a gravity wave, barely detectable but all-pervasive. Reflect: Her *Preface,* Part 1, directly introduces Part 2, *The Walrus.* So far, so good. Then, she gives *no* introduction to Jillian's *Confession*, Part 3, and only *two small paragraphs* introduce Jillian's *Journal,* Part 4. Nicolette requires *only one small paragraph* to introduce me, in *PSLS*, Part 5. Nothing more! The short preface, plus three paragraphs. It is astonishing that a structure of this complexity stands! She found its center of gravity.

Nicolette's words constitute but a tiny fraction of *The Bequest's* entire corpus. Once, during the hypnogogic spinout resulting from my mistakenly having taken a second sleeping pill, my impaired consciousness mused; 'Was Nicolette really both "Jillian," and "William," under a mask?' Did she write the whole thing? All of it? She wrote the whole thing! No, not possible!'

Well, had not Jillian interacted with me over years in real life, and had not William also in fact been my student, I would have thought so. My reverie was merely the musing of a superannuated literature teacher, but I want you to begin to think like this, to be musicians "bending" notes, bending perspectives to intensify effect.

----I need another stretch. ...Ooow ...Arthritis. ...Among other things. Don't get old. ...Ooof. Okay, back to work.----

Oh, no, there's the bell.

Lecture 2: Overview of *The Bequest*

Some images are *eidetic*. They are unforgettable. Example: In the movie of Anthony Burgess' novel, *A Clockwork Orange*, a prison warden observes the anti-hero, the prisoner, a psychopath, a killer, earnestly reading the New Testament in the prison library. A non-recidivist success story? An early release maybe? Very good. The warden is pleased.

Seamlessly zooming in to the exact moment that the prisoner was intent on, the next scene shows Jesus being flogged on the way to crucifixion. And what do we see? Who do we see flogging the staggering Jesus? Our friend the prisoner! Smiling. Having a grand ole fantasy. It is only a tiny step further to imagine our hero swelling towards erection at his soul-satisfying act of whipping Jesus.

The point? Can we tell from the outside what is going on at the center of the soul? Can souls ever really interpenetrate?

As David Gilmour and Roger Waters, the Pink Floyd poets, both say and sing, "So ...you think you can tell ...heaven from hell

...a smile from a veil?" Perspective and belief bend almost everything. Reality is rarely glimpsed in full. It is bent and colored by these lenses. But the distortions of sensory and moral ambiguity *are* occasionally resolved, and a more accurate reality is perceived.

Then the question becomes: Can it be sustained? The shared reality can be sustained if —and this is the big *if*— both parties, or all parties, risk being honest and vulnerable. At its heart, this is what *The Walrus* is "about." But do not mistake being open and vulnerable with a "kumbaya" experience. Quite the opposite. Honesty is fraught: it puts the whole relationship at risk. It *can* be wonderful, but it is scary.

We all *now* know that *The Walrus* was William's play, but we did *not* know this on first reading it. At least *I* didn't. Originally, the title Jillian proposed for her play —so I was led to believe at the time— was *The Willing Interpenetration of Souls.* The title had to be changed.

On the content level, *The Walrus* asks, among other questions: On what basis is trust established? And, on what basis should sex —sex as an expression of love, not recreational sex— be included? And, if society forbids an honest discussion of an issue, how honest can people be in revealing their innermost selves? This is dramatized in the main character's conflict: should she take refuge in received values or dare she risk growing beyond her reference group, beyond her parents, and even beyond the limits of her own imagined Self?

The writer's job was to demonstrate the soul-altering *effect* of a deep love experience. The writer had to show the character *experiencing* a new way of being. We become convinced of this change by Jillian's increasingly direct speech and confident demeanor, and in her growing intellectual sophistication.

For next time, your assignment is to take any sequence of four to six lines in *The Walrus* —not more— and write out what the characters were really feeling, hoping for, trying to do. What was felt *between* the lines?

The Walrus is a subtle *cri de coeur* from its author to young women —and to men, especially young men, if they have the slightest interest in learning from it— as emotional-sexual guidance. It is one roadmap for male–female lovemaking and love. It is also obviously a challenge to received societal prescriptions and unexamined personal beliefs. As playwright, Linden, (whether William or Jillian), had to dramatize alternatives to conventional expectations. The transformation of the lead character had to be delivered via the interplay of the dialog and actions. The dramatization had to be powerful to be convincing.

Two other major characters appear in *The Walrus*. They were necessary permutations. Having four main characters allowed him/her to dramatize alternatives. The four-way character-prism allows —and forces— the reader into a rounded consideration of the intense moral, personal, social issues at stake in the play.

Each character's voice is distinctive. William and Roberta are distinct, but they sound psychologically kindred, and this implicitly supports the claim that they had much in common by mindset, personality and even defenses. Caitlin, character four, sounds somewhat different than her sister but only *somewhat* different. They are sisters but not kindred souls. It is Jillian's voice that changes most because she undergoes the most character–changing experiences. It is a major theme that as she develops her independence she finds her voice! Voice is a keyword. How Jillian sounds in ACTs I and II contrasts markedly to how she sounds in ACTs III and IV. More about this *pas de quatre* character development in the next lectures.

As you were reading it, did you know did you wonder who the author of *The Walrus* was? Did you know from whose point of view were the events unfolding? Could you tell? ...Hers? ...His? ...Both? ...Equally?

As we read *The Walrus* we experience the dramatic flow from an indeterminate central place of soul interpenetration! Yin *and* Yang rotating around the Wu Shi centerpoint, female and male, potential fullness and fullness morphing into one another. The angled planes of *Les Demoiselles* giving rise to a sense of three-dimensionality from a two-dimensional surface! A richer *inter*penetration of viewer, subject matter and artist, or in the present case, reader, subject matter and author.

The Bequest requires focus and refocusing. What was the timeline of the events? How old was Nicolette when she created the framing architecture? How old were the other characters, especially Jillian, at the time of the events in the plotline? And who is speaking to whom, especially when this, *PSLS,* is added to the mix? Through her use of these lectures Nicolette forces the reader to reframe the timeline once again. And time —the fourth dimension— becomes an element in her story. To illustrate, Jillian's *Confession,* Part 3, requires the reader to consider her growth well beyond her original transformation in *The Walrus.* And Jillian's *Journal*, Part 4, evidences her further growth; it having been practice for her to gain the confidence to write for real. We can surmise from text that what Nicolette as teenager saw Jillian typing was *My Other Confession.* Nothing else makes sense. I'll illustrate further.

A "close reading" of text means that you take every fact and check its integration within the overall fabric. There are only five candidates here: *The Confession* a, b or c and Jillian's *Journal* which has two sections, items 1-6, and item 7, titled, *My Other Confession*. We know from text *when* Jillian wrote parts 3b and 3c, in one smooth flow, untrammeled by doubt, during the afternoon of our last meeting. So that eliminates them. Next, items 1-6, of her *Journal*, stipulates certain facts within both *The Confession* and *The Walrus*, so therefore they, items 1-6, could not have been what Nicolette had seen Jillian writing. The only remaining candidates are 3a, her Introduction to *The Confession* and item 7, her *Other Confession*. It just feels right to suspect that Jillian had prepared 3a shortly before our last meeting, 3b, and that she kept it warm on a back burner in the run-up to our meeting. 3b and c mesh so fluidly with 3a, that all three read like a work in need of no correction, like a composition of Mozart's, a work perfect from inception.

This leaves only Item 7. Jillian must have been going through the throes of her *Other Confession*. This thesis is made more compelling if we recall Nicolette's age when Jillian refused to let her read the material she was working on! Assuming this line of reasoning is correct, then one further deduction is required. I conclude that Jillian wrote her *Other Confession* and hadn't decided where to place it in her journal; had put question marks around it. Nicolette, as Uber-author, placed it at the back end of Jillian's *Journal* for her. Items 1-6 of her *Journal* would thereby serve as an intellectual and comedic entertainment, a fun interlude, lulling and soothing the unsuspecting reader prior to the heartbreak of Jillian's, *Other Confession*. Nicolette's sequencing "bends" the notes. The strategic placement intensifies the emotional effect.

By illustrating this close reading from text I hope to encourage you to be flexible when composing your own works. I am virtually certain that Nicolette did revise the sequence of Part 4's constituent items, but I do enjoy the trace of uncertainty. Any great work should have an element of mystery, be that work visual, musical or written. You know that I could have asked the author directly, and she would have told me. But that would have been cheating. Why should I have an advantage that you don't enjoy? I am not posing as a divine. We, as artists, struggle to get the flow right. Nicolette had to work on placing Item 7. In my opinion, the *Other Confession* had to come *after* the other *Journal* items.

Back to *The Walrus*. Was it Jillian or William who wrote it? Jillian had originally claimed authorship of *The Walrus* and for decades I believed her misrepresentation of that "fact." Yet, that proves the point! The omniscient narrator perspective is so unobtrusively buried in the Wu Shi centerpoint that the individual consciousness of *both* characters is retained while both are subsumed into a double and evolving consciousness. Isn't that how we feel when we are in love? Souls interpenetrating willingly?

Not until the Introduction to *The Confession,* 3a, does Jillian permit us to know whose play it really was. That the writer —whichever of them it was— is capable of suspending the reader in this haze of uncertainty is testament to the degree of soul interpenetration exhibited in *The Walrus.*

My Confession, Part 3b, is Jillian's direct bequest to her esteemed Creative Writing instructor ...*moi*. She had confessed to the reader just previously in 3a what he, that is I, did not yet know and was about to find out. By confessing to the reader first, she *induces* the reader to be more acutely aware of what she is doing to Morton. The reader is now ahead of Morton. Despite the whirling yet entertaining colloquial-speech dialog in 3b, the reader is focused on Jillian's goal. She has induced them to be thinking, 'How will Jillian do what she wishes to do?'

In fact, she lets Morton know pieces of the truth, leading him with a trail of breadcrumbs, her "mistakes." She recovers from them and continues her cat-and-mouse induction game until Morton forces a clarification. Jillian has accomplished her purpose.

Skipping to the Reprise, 3c, Jillian exposes another layer, the *almost* full truth. Yet even there, she tantalized him —me— with one more layer of truth about to be "illuminated," and *that* would happen when Morton received the final draft of *The Confession* along with *The Walrus*.

Your indulgence here for a very long aside and a warning.

Jillian had offered that I resembled a combination of Mr. Magoo and Moses-with-the-tablets. A combination of Christopher

Reeves and George Clooney is more accurate and I'm sure that those of you who want an "A" in this course assent to that. A show of hands, please....

Now ...stay *particularly* attentive ...slap your minds again! In reference to the little farce above, if I inserted "smile" into the text —right here, as if I were writing a play or story, for example, "the class smiles"— that would be an instance of second-order metatext, a meta-metatextual devise. Follow? Fascinating maybe, but I distinctly advise you *against* orders of metatext. The work becomes needlessly difficult, tedious. Even a great writer like Nabokov got lost in the forest of Meta, as he did in *Ada.* Don't do it!

Now and additionally, since I despise when educators breezily profess things, such as my foregoing remark about getting lost in metatext, and they implicitly expect students to take their word for it, I owe it to you to demonstrate *how* a writer can get lost, not just declare it. Ready? Minds awake?

Here goes. First, I defy you to find one *Walrus* line or even one *induced* feeling or thought that sounds like it could not have been written by Jillian from her point of view! She had in fact declared that she would write a play: ACT III Scene 2, lines 12 and 13. "*I'll* write a play and my play will be about *love*. I *will*. I'll start *tomorrow*." Now just suppose —for fun— that I informed you that Jillian *had* written *The Walrus* and that her *Confession* was the second part of a self-imposed imaginative exercise. She *could* have written it. I believed for years that she had!

Second —and here's the payoff line— if Nicolette, from her artistic standpoint, had felt it made sense to introduce yet another level of complexity into *this* novel, *she* would have lost her way! The storyline would have become mired in ambiguity. What benefit would further uncertainty yield? To show off? To perplex the reader? The reader would get entangled for no purpose! Happily, Nicolette did not needlessly complicate her fiction which is already quite complex. My point in a nutshell? Metatext without necessity leads nowhere. *Quod Erat Demonstrandum.* Q.E.D.

Returning, ...Jillian's *Confession*, Part 3, requires high power magnification and I will examine that Part microscopically in Lecture 7. But for now I simply point out that Jillian's, *Introduction*, 3a, is truly elegant writing. It is emeritus professor-worthy. But elegance aside, you must recognize that it is an elaborate intertextual riff on Joyce! Two long, multi-claused sentences mirror the rhythm pattern at the beginning of *Ulysses*. Jillian even managed to metabolize Joyce's word, "intoned," authentically for her own purposes, which intensifies her homage to him right down to the level of diction!

She then drafts Professor Seiden, Morton, me, into the story as a character and at *that* moment she switches from narration to drama! Notice a loop, a recursion? Nicolette had done exactly that —switch from narration to drama, twice!— in the middle of her *Preface*. From our perspective —*The Bequest*'s framing arc— Nicolette's device silently functions as foreshadowing, while Jillian's use of the switch is inadvertently a recursion simply due to the fact that that's the way we come across her switch in text. From text we also know that Jillian wrote *The Confession* long before Nicolette undertook her creative enterprise. You see why if you don't grasp the timeframe there is no way you can walk away from this book feeling that you comprehend the whole thing? I've needed three lectures on the *Preface* plus the overall architecture of *The Bequest as-a-whole* for that reason: it's rounded, musical, recursive complexity.

We should ask, Is this switching from narrative to drama merely a case of "like mother-like daughter," or "life imitating art?" No, again. It is an instance of *intertext*, internal intertext in this case. The "conversation" is between Nicolette, as writer, and her mother, as writer. Nicolette, is also using the switch to subliminally sensitize the reader to a second level of enjoyment by pre-figuring, foreshadowing, Jillian's technique of switching from narrative to drama, in Part 3 of *The Bequest*.

The Bequest demands multiple cognitive shifts not only within the text, but also on the meta level. The four sides of her novel are positioned to encourage, and force, the reader to construct a more full-dimensional mental representation of the work as a whole, to grasp it in the round, like the angling planes of *Les Demoiselles,* or the Tower.

Bear with me.... *The Bequest* is a Moebius tesseract! Definition: Moebius [strip], a continuous single-sided surface formed by rotating one end of a strip through 180 degrees and joining it to the other end. Definition: Tesseract, a four-dimensional imaginary object that has the same relationship to a cube as a cube does to a square.

Topmost level consideration: does reading any novel —including this one— delight us and make us feel something more saliently? Does it bring into emotional focus something that we didn't grasp before reading it? That, as I see it, is the job of literature. Nicolette's complex structure is, in the final analysis, about nothing less than an attempt to wrestle with a universal moral question while at the same time having fun with the sheer sonic enchantment of words and the visual images they can create.

Back to ground level: Jillian's two-level shadow play with Morton can teach you timing, that is, when to bring in what you wish the reader to know or wish to induced them to think and feel. As Jillian had done with me in 3b, you must put the reader through a sequence of events to have them feel and think about the transpiring events, their meanings and implications. In her play, Jillian assessed Morton's mental status to see if he was still capable of apprehending the gift she wished to give him. Through their dialog, she evaluates Morton's short- and long-term memory. Via both her inadvertent mistakes as well as her purposeful "mistakes," she tests his mental agility, his capacity for humor, and his ability to focus and to refocus. All this is done playfully and most of all, respectfully. She could have halted or retreated at any time. Morton catches on though; he still has his marbles. He tries to get her to fess up, to tell him what was really on her mind. Jillian lets him catch her up to a point, but at the end of 3b she whipsaws Morton's focus and of course the reader's, to exert her leadership within this intricate weaving. Never had Morton heard her speak so authoritatively! He was delighted. Her growth astonished him.

Meta level: *My Confession*, section b of Jillian's *Confession*, metabolized their contemporaneous conversation into dialog.

Remember we are still analyzing *The Bequest*'s **macrostructure**. (Before proceeding, I apologize for the density of this lecture, but the material demands it. I am acutely conscious of time and I would have shortened this critique if it were possible, but it is not. Relax. Upcoming lectures will be somewhat less dense.)

Leaving aside the tender-torrid love affair of the two main characters, *The Walrus* grapples with broader social and moral issues. These issues had to be presented in an, "Oh my god, I don't believe it!" forceful way. Had the writing been less passionate Jillian's mind-changing experiences would not have been convincing to her, nor to us. Most importantly, had the love affair been presented from only one of their points of view, the reader would have turned off because the play's storyline would have seemed prepackaged, slanted, "tendentious," to use the word that I had used with Jillian decades earlier.

Also note Nicolette's sincerity when she says early on: "I love that conversation. The level of respect and honesty, the giving as well as the not backing down." Actually this quite a bold affirmation because by giving this appraisal of the Morton-Jillian dialog she risks offending the reader who might be thinking, 'While praising her mother is she also covertly praising herself?' Her opinion risks sounding self-congratulatory. Nicolette knew this, but she just tells it like it is. She simply vouches for it.

Is this simply idiosyncrasy? "Style?" A stylistic misstep? Again, no, it is neither self-serving grandiosity nor ingenuousness because Nicolette is grooming the reader for the intense level of honesty that saturates *The Walrus*. Her naïve-appearing sincerity functions as induction. She is preparing the reader for the unprecedented and, for many readers, hard-to-take level of honesty coming up next. Throughout *The Walrus,* three of the four characters are that way, and by the end of the play, so too is Jillian. All four risk truth-telling. That is what is so refreshing about the play. It is challenging and at moments even brutally honest, but it is breathtakingly beautiful in its honesty.

I wish now to halo a second eidetic moment; one that is Shakespeareanly perfect! It is from Nicole Krauss' unforgettable novel, *The History of Love.* Jillian reminds us of it when she brings it up in conversation with me in 3b of her *Confession.* The line relates to Krauss' hero, Leo —courageous and pathetic Leo— who finds a book ...that has *his* name on it! And in fact, it is something he *had* written, decades ago! He had no idea it still *existed*! He thought it had been lost. He had no idea *why* it existed where he found it! He had not even known it had been *typed up*! Typed up *and* translated into English! Krauss bolds the sentence. "**Could I be famous without knowing it**?" Howlingly funny and howlingly painful. Agonizingly beautiful. Perfect! Both the moment and the sentence. Unforgettable. Eidetic!

Speaking again of perfect moments, or at least of apt ones, could there be a more apt time than right now to discuss the author's name? Most readers will think, "So Nicolette Linden wrote this story. ...So what?" But some will think about it, and those who do, will be rewarded. They will be tickled by the fact that Jillian named her offspring, Nicolette, little Nicole. For the reader, then,

Jillian naming her daughter Nicolette implicitly dramatizes how important Nicole Krauss was to Jillian. Q.E.D.

Her name is an instructive instance of the writer, Nicolette, giving no hint to the reader of what the other writer, Jillian, her mother, was doing by so naming her. Nicolette knew, of course — how could she not?!— but she lets the reader figure things out and enjoy the connection for themselves. You should do the same. There is no heavy-handed authorial "signing." Flaubert first showed us how to do this in *Madame Bovary*. You recall that wonderful scene in which Emma and her lover are having a fine time of it in the carriage while, "*Race porcine*" and, "*Race bovine*" are barked in the background. No wink–wink to the audience. My take home message to you: Trust your reader. You can demand work from them so long as the writing flows and is meaningful. Krauss did it. William did it. Jillian did it. Nicolette did it. You do it; or try to.

In summary, *The Bequest* as–a–whole combines qualities that appear only very infrequently: 1) entertaining, rapid, absorbing dialog while simultaneously requiring considerable cognitive work on the reader's part; 2) accessible language with depth of themes; and 3) dynamic, meaningful interplay of characters.

Thus far, I've been discussing mainly macrostructure. Halfway through next lecture, I will shift focus to micro-structure.

Oh, there's the bell! ...Wonderful. I am very tired.

Lecture 3: (A double lecture) Macrostructure continued and, micro-structural examination of *The Preface*

Nicolette Linden's *The Bequest* should not work! It subsumes two very distinct and separately compelling works by two different authors. *The Walrus*, her father's, occurs within the Theater of the Mind. Her mother's, *The Confession* —that panini of story-play-story which I referenced earlier— would have no relation to anything if not read in conjunction with *The Walrus*. It would be untethered, merely a beautiful but rogue piece of writing. So those two works, like good parents, have a correlated and symbiotic relationship. They required Nicolette to imagine an overarching entity, a fully functional new "organism" which she "gave birth" to. And that project had to be both crystal clear and yet complex enough to metabolize those "parental" works into the "grandchild" organism. And, as a wild card mutation, she spliced these lectures into the "gene pool," for good measure.

Now, you know that I like to walk you around the corner and then bring you back to the original spot. You thereby gain an enhanced perspective. So ...a metallurgist friend of mine informed me that the tensile strength of spider silk is five times stronger than the same weight of steel. With her nearly invisible narrative silk, Nicolette braces all sides of her Eiffel Tower to each other. I refer here to her tying together William's work with Jillian's. Recall the timeline. Jillian produced her *Confession*, Part 3, decades after William's *Walrus*. Sometime later still, Nicolette —after she has read them more than a hundred times and feels compelled to change her career path— hoists these works at ninety degrees to each other, like the Tower. She has found the center of gravity for her imaginative acrobatics!

Drilling down to specifics: her *Preface*, Part 1, braces with Parts 2, 3 and 5. When you go back to re-read *The Bequest*, you will recognize how Nicolette had been lashing the sides together since the beginning. *The Preface,* like a plug entering an electrical socket, joins directly with *The Walrus, Part2*. Within her *Preface*, the *Morton and Jillian Discuss the Title* dialog ties together with Jillian's work, Part 3. The same dialog also winches this, *PSLS,* Part 5, to the narrative corpus. By co-opting me as a character into her *Preface,* and by using and subsuming Jillian's *Confession* —in which I also appear— she ties together and anchors into solid earth the various Parts of her novel. The four parts are grounded; they are bound together with stronger-than-steel cross-bracing. The reader Is empowered to solve the equations for the three-dimensional architecture of her tower. But they have to work for it. There is more interstitial lacing and lashing but this is enough microscopy to get you started.

I am deconstructing both spinning pinwheels, Nicolette's and Jillian's —each a *tour de force* of intertext and metatextual play— to prod you to write adventurously. Risk it. If you have something authentic to say, experiment to find the right key to say it in. That advice is for your future. For our present purpose, keep the framing arc of this novel uppermost in mind.

Returning ...in the preceding lecture, I had been talking about Jillian and how she had beguiled Morton. *She* led *him* in her *Confession*! Even reading it now, it dazzles. She made purposeful evasions, as William had done with her in *The Walrus*. As writers, they are having a "dialog," Jillian honoring William through imitation.

The use of purposeful evasions and "mistakes" evinces subtle intertext. Subtle, because recursion and intertext do not only have to be in diction or theme; here Jillian's writing is intertext by *technique* —imitation of style— and it would not be detected by the casual reader. But not you ...now. James Joyce did this to the most elaborate degree, but I dare not digress. I will detail Joyce's imitations of style in later lectures. Talk about *tours de force.*

Full disclosure: William had also been student of mine about five years before Jillian. He, too, did not go into writing. Jillian made genuine mistakes talking with me, these due to the cognitive load of complex plot organization she was secretly weaving. Imagine ...she was consciously intending to use our ongoing dialog while she was talking with me! She was in the plot on surface level but also navigating from the bridge, viewing us from above, sitting in a Director's chair, like Hamlet listening from the third dimension.

For homework, choose any one page of *My Confession,* 3b, and in one paragraph delineate how she makes the reader wait —as she had forced me to wait— until the *Reprise,* 3c, to understand what she was doing. ...All right, all right ...two paragraphs; two *non*-Proustian paragraphs, please. Practice being concise.

Jillian passionately wanted Morton to understand something. Above and beyond that though, she wanted to promote the reader to become doubly-conscious. Her work *forces* the reader to have that experience because the dialog itself loops around with many comedic stagger-steps interposed between the seriousness of her purpose. The Jillian-Morton conversation sounds so authentic because it contains the little disconnects and reconnects of ordinary speech.

Nicolette too, wishes to promote —and force— the reader to become doubly-conscious. The term I prefer for consciousness-of-consciousness is "Awareness." Awareness is the experiential brocade that results from identification with Self and Other, from cognitive shuttling between perspectives. It is *interpersonal* depth perception, analogous to *spatial* depth perception which arises from *binocularity*. "Bi." Consciousness from more than one's own point of view. Roundedness. *Les Demoiselles.* The Tower.

Even with Jillian's confession beforehand in 3a, the reader cannot anticipate the purpose of the dialog's interlocking construction. Jillian has positioned herself into a contortion, a conundrum that seems impossible to get out of: present tense dialog, past tense allusions, a future tense declaration within both 3b and 3c. But get out of it she does! The writing is as close as writing can come to being in the picture–plane of the present, and, as you know, storytelling necessarily occurs in the past. But *My Confession* occurs in the present! It is a jewel, a diamond set between the baguettes of 3a and 3c. Even when you re-read it, and therefore know where it is heading, it has the electric vivacity of the Present. Jillian wanted to induce the reader to be doubly-conscious. So does Nicolette. That is the *purpose* of the interlocking construction! Heightened consciousness. Awareness. This is storytelling *au jus d'acide lysergique*.

Yes, dear Jillian had previously misled me by claiming authorship of *The Walrus*. And yes, there is a spot in *The Walrus* that I might have puzzled over —which spot Jillian explains directly to the reader in her *Introduction*, 3a— but she was a recent past student at the time when she misled me, and her need for me, heightened so drastically by the tragedy, made me fuzzy. Avuncularly fuzzy. I missed it. Even so, *The Walrus* works so well that, like the loose threads in *Hamlet,* it didn't matter for us as readers. During the *My Confession* conversation, I continued to take for granted that *The Walrus* was Jillian's work. Only a hint in 3b suggested differently, and then later, when I was forced, happily, to read Jillian's full *Confession, 3a, b and c,* and therefore, to re-re-read *The Walrus,* did I learn the truth, the full truth. Yet still more truth awaited me before all was illuminated. *That* came with Nicolette's document, her book. Interlocking circles within circles. Orbiting pinwheels, both Jillian's and Nicolette's. Amazing, and so beautiful.

In her *Preface* to *The Bequest,* Nicolette recounts a dialog with her mother during which Jillian insisted that the reason for the cited quote from The Beatles would become clear to those readers who wondered about it. Jillian *wanted* her readers to puzzle over it. She wanted her readers to do this work by themselves without her signing to them, to engage their curiosity actively. But Nicolette knew that the reader needed *some* clues, some landmarks. She knew the significance of the Morton–Jillian discussion. Technically, this was foreshadowing and it is also another example of intertextual dialog between Nicolette and Jillian. She used the salvaged Morton–Jillian discussion to alert the reader, to suggest that something was up with the absurd title, something obscure but important. Good call, Nicolette.

The question of the title was absolutely essential. *Morton and Jillian Discuss the Title* could *not* have been left out. Without it, *The Walrus* as title, is absurd. "I am he as you are he as you are me, and we are all together." Is this nonsense? It certainly sounds like it. But, not in this case, however. The line is celebrating a moment of soul interpenetration. Two happy lovers feeling as one, suffused with love and trust, revolving around each other, the world revolving around them. A healthy merger state, not a confusional one. Jillian, on the other hand, could not have used it within her *Confession* since it would have entangled the reader in noncontributory complexity. You know, as writers, we must discard as much as we put in. Jillian applied her scissors. Nicolette's stroke of genius was how she repurposed it; like Shakespeare repurposing and expanding the *Ur*-Hamlet material.

Nicolette knew that the *M and J* discussion had to be woven in *somewhere*. But where? She knew that the reader needed preparatory inoculation prior to the emotional tempest looming just around the corner in Part 2, *The Walrus*. She used the dialog in "*Morton and Jillian Discuss the Title*" as foreshadowing. It gives the reader a reference point, a landmark. It allows the reader to orient themselves and later to re-orient themselves as they weave their way through *The Bequest*'s spherical Moebius loops.

Perspectives. As I believe I said in Lecture 1, reading *The Bequest*, especially *The Walrus*, is like trying to drink from a fire hose. It is an almost-living Rubik's cube or, better, a Rubik's *sphere* of perspectives. It demands continuous cognitive re-contextualizing. It cannot be read slowly. Not the first few times. And in her *Confession,* Jillian weaves a Moebius strip of present, past and future tenses. They twist around and into each other. She incorporated our in-the-moment dialog into a future-oriented declaration, which declaration she promptly fulfilled in the then–

present reality. Mercifully, comedy does leaven seriousness, but the dialog presses relentlessly forward.

And *Brava!* to Nicolette, for integrating it all.

----Stretch break time!----

With all of the foregoing as preparation, we can finally examine Nicolette's *Preface* in micro.

Right at the outset and easy to miss, Nicolette gives the first of her many loving homages, this one to John Fowles. He opens *The Magus*, with the main character saying:

"I was born in 1927, the only child of middle-class parents, both English, and themselves born in the grotesquely elongated shadow, which they never rose sufficiently above history to leave, of that monstrous dwarf Queen Victoria."

Nicolette's opens her novel just *before* she was born!

"When I was an embryo, my mother did not know she was pregnant, and my father ...well, he's another story. Actually, no, he's very much a part of this story."

Nicolette is tipping her hat to Fowles, honoring him and competing with him. Structurally, the opening bars of Nicolette's overture are veiled intertext: she is loosely imitating the rhythm pattern —the prosody— of Fowles' great book. It is such a tender and playful subsurface homage, and it works within her storyline.

On ground level, the writer immediately offers herself in a confidential manner. But just as with *The Magus,* where the casual reader has no idea how much work was going to be required to enjoy *that* novel, the reader of this novel has no idea of what is in store for them. Hers, like Fowles', is not just another novel.

Nicolette follows with the second of a one-two punch, another homage to Fowles, this one even more subtle. Re-read Fowles' paragraph above and immediately read the first line of *The Preface*'s paragraph three. The prosody of this sentence is, again, almost identical to the first sentence in *The Magus*! It works, it flows, it is beautiful, and it is so easy to miss. So while Nicolette is telling you about her mother's personality, she is also doing something else. Veiled intertext. As writers and readers you should be sensitive to these echoes. They enrich the symphony.

Nicolette then gives a quick dotted-line sketch about her father. In constructing *The Bequest* she had to have asked herself, 'Am I equal in imaginative power to my father and my mother?' 'Can I create a coherent framework to govern those two torrential rivers?'

By the way, I purposely skipped over her one-sentence second paragraph: "By the way, call me Nicolette." With this, she straightforwardly invites the reader into conversation with her. Innocent. Even naïve, maybe. But —however innocuous this sounds superficially— it is an unmistakable echo from the opening of Melville's, *Moby Dick,* "Call me Ishmael." Veiled intertext again. She is tickling the reader's intuitive funny bone; Fowles, Fowles again, Melville. ...Others? Who else? The alert reader has to now be thinking, 'What is she up to?' and, 'Maybe Nicolette is more sophisticated than she appears?' That Nicolette is capable of being on two levels at once, namely, both ingenuous and artful, has been induced in the readers mind.

On ground level she introduces the characters within an ordinary family context; honest, simple, and believable. But, on the meta level, she will shortly make herself vanish from the narrative. Then later, like a magician, she reappears. She is a *magus*, whose legerdemain integrates her parents' writings as well as this critique into an organic whole! *That* requires *some* imagination. *Some* mental prestidigitation!

Back to micro-structure. In paragraph 3, she gives a heartfelt precis of her mother's personality and she supplies an example. The accuracy of her precis resonates at once. Nicolette has established herself as a trustworthy narrator. We know through their dialog in the *Preface*, that the two women —or at that moment, a mid-teen and her mother— respect and love each other. She had already portrayed her mother's personality and emotional intelligence by describing her mother's action when helping her pack for college. Nicolette gave her reaction to that action in the then–present, and also retroflexively from the now–future. Again, an alternation of tenses and perspectives. Good so far. Simple, charming.

And, not so simple. She requires the reader to start weaving timeframes. The reader will shortly witness a daughter–mother debate, an emotional snag. Momentarily leaving aside the material causing the snag, what could be more ordinary? Again, ordinary, realistic and lovely. But under the surface Nicolette is again ensnaring the reader. She is inducing the reader to ask, Why? Why this snag?

At that moment the reader gets whooshed into the complexity! Nicolette's mother, Jillian, figures centrally in the upcoming *Walrus,* and again as she reaches her fullest maturity in *The Confession.* I'll return to this shortly.

Fairness now requires Nicolette to describe her father. She knows that if she doesn't supply something, the alert reader will suspect that she may be planning to have him make a surprise entrance later and she doesn't want this. She doesn't want the reader to dangle or to anticipate her. Yet the observations about her father cannot come only from her mother, they must also be reflections from others. So, paragraph 4: Nicolette refers to her cousin, to his understanding of her father, and to a friend of her father's. These familial and friend references are again charming, but they are only somewhat satisfying because they are not dramatized but merely declared by the cousin and the friend. Reader's reaction? Tentative approval perhaps, but also, perhaps, mild annoyance. This mild annoyance is intended. Induction again. To provoke curiosity. Will the father be fleshed out more? When?

Right away. Paragraph 5. Four short sentences. But therein, what a claim about her father is made by her mother! Her father is not fully fleshed out, but his large place on the canvas is outlined.

Next, she introduces another character, Morton —that's right, *me*— in order to set the legal background for *The Bequest.* This fact is text in Part 3, Jillian's *Confession*, and becomes metatext in this, Part 5, *Professor Seiden's Last Seminar.*

Nicolette next gives the reader a sniff, a hint, of the two documents' complexity. If Morton could not succeed in helping Jillian get the documents published —as we are informed in this paragraph— then the rejection by the publishing houses gives circumstantial evidence of the ambiguity in characterizing the documents' genre.

Nicolette is prefacing *The Walrus,* the intense second part of *The Bequest* that concerns her father, her mother, their intimate interactions, and especially, her mother's growth. It also explores many permutations from the perspective of their friends, characters three and four. About these next two characters Jillian was highly ambivalent, even distinctly negative, but she undergoes a change of mind and heart as drastic as Elizabeth Bennett's about Mr. Darcy in *Pride and Prejudice.* Her growth is manifested in ACTs III and IV of *The Walrus.*

Let's refocus. As-a-whole, *The Bequest* contains three major Parts: *The Walrus, My Confession*, [3b], and this, my critique of her novel. A framing story was absolutely needed to metamorphose the major Parts into a novel. As-a-whole it *is* a novel; it is not drama; nor a prose poem —as I had wanted to argue with Jillian, just for fun— nor is it an essay. The dramatic intensity lives in each part, but Nicolette had to integrate the parts into a whole. This was the test of *her* creativity. This was the imaginative leap that she had to make. She had to make them into a novel. All parts must cohere. However defined, the work must *flow*.

How does a writer integrate such disparate works into one framework? She did it by finding the painting's central vanishing point, the singularity of emptiness and potential fullness, the Wu Shi centerpoint. She did it by being empty and distant while also being on intimate terms with the reader: Nicolette is empty of egotism and she never waves to the reader how important she is to the construction of the integrated story. She is nearly invisible. *Indeed*, she utters so *few* words as narrator that it is miraculous that her framework supports a novel of this complexity.

She also maintains her distance from the underlying volcanic Yin and Yang of the Jillian-William love story. Other than remarking on how powerfully the bequeathed documents impacted her, she makes no commentary about that material. And the impact of *The Walrus* and *The Confession* is vetted by her action: she gave up her profession to become a writer, "to bring them into the light," to deliver them.

As to the title: Nicolette herself is an embodiment of "bequests." She inherited much from her mother via Jillian's mothering, of course, as well as Jillian's bequest of the central documents; much physically and spiritually from her father; and the additional bequest via Morton who was the intermediate custodian of them. Intricacy filigreed into intricacy. Recursion interpolating into recursion. What better name?

Returning to ground level ...an abrupt turn follows. Nicolette was *not* allowed to read this material. What a stunning declaration! None of it. Her Mom informs her that her work, *The Confession*, "would make no sense" without knowing *The Walrus*. And Nicolette is not allowed to read *that* until she reaches a certain age. Age thirty. *What*? This is *nonsensical*! Even shocking. Why? Why not! The reader too is shocked. This reaction is precisely what Nicolette wants. She is preparing the reader for the turbulence ahead. *Thirty*? What kind of stuff lies ahead? Why does her Mom not give her more satisfactory answers? The writer wants the reader to have these questions. This is craft: induction.

Jillian knew what she was doing with Nicolette, and now Nicolette, as writer, knows what she is doing to the reader. These parallel loops, greatly separated in time, are stitches in the fabric: this is how Nicolette constructed her edifice, composed her symphony. As writers, the sequence of changes you wish to put the reader through is critical. If well done, the read will be vivid. And if done really well, unforgettable. Nicolette knew that the reader needed a speed-bump warning. She is trying to slow down and frame the reader's reading of *The Walrus* because the material is so impassioned and controversial, that she herself was denied access to it even though her mother respected, loved and admired her! We, the reader, are now provoked and our seatbelt is fastened.

An aside. We get the first of glimmers of Jillian's shall I say, love affair, with *Hamlet*. Nicolette had felt put-off by her Mom's answers, to which Jillian replied, "He hinted, he didn't explain." As writer of the superstructure, Nicolette provides this *hint*, this tease, to signal that many harmonics from *Hamlet* weave through Jillian's document. In Jillian's work, however, they weave mostly subtly, subterraneanly. Most readers will not even realize the seismic rumblings, but Jillian wanted the reader to enjoy the "under–harmonics," so she playfully unveils them in the first part of her *Journal,* Items 1-6.

Ground level again: Nicolette had tried to overcome her mother by logic. She references, as a last resort —both of them being intellectuals— two other of Shakespeare's plays that she knows her mother knows well. But to no avail. Sorry, ... no deal. Nyet! Game over.

Note too that the entirety of Jillian's *Journal,* Part 4, is an extensive homage to James Joyce. It mirrors Joyce's marvelous and first-of-its-kind chapter in *Ulysses* wherein, incredibly, Leopold Bloom is catechized about everything he did, thought about, and fantasized during his daylong odyssey around Dublin. Jillian is having an intertextual conversation with Joyce. Her *Journal* items 1–6 are intertext via style and diction. And item 7, her *Other Confession,* is a brave remembrance of things past; things that she sincerely wished she didn't have to remember and confess.

Now let's refocus on Nicolette's framing architecture. After a miniscule introduction, she embeds the only other known sample of Jillian's writing, her *Journal,* as Part 4 of *The Bequest.* Nicolette salvaged and repurposed this rarity and made it part of her own work.

At first, the *Journal* probably seemed a distracting throw-in. It is not however, because it shows Jillian's further growth into writerhood. Nicolette knew that by including it, the harmonics from both her father's and her mother's verbal symphonies would be amplified.

On its metalevel, Jillian's *Journal* is a loving cascade of intertextual homages to Joyce and to Shakespeare. And she had given the most profound homage to Pink Floyd in her heartfelt **Advance Directive** at the end of 3c.

Nicolette's use of her mother's *Journal* also functions as a wah-wah pedal in that it adds resonance and depth to the reader's experience. The reverbs also surreptitiously remind us of the theatricality of Jillian's final moments — which we prefer not to think about.

And don't overlook the word, "magnificently," within Nicolette's argument with her Mom. It will reoccur later, in *The Walrus*, several times, and very importantly. It could even qualify as a keyword, to add to the four that William itemized in his Notes. Nicolette is stitching the *Preface* together with the fabric of *The Walrus* by foreshadowing the repetition of that word. Her stitching is so subtle that it passes under the radar of most readers. They will feel a connection, a coherence, without being able to identify the reason for feeling it. Jillian, who liked to sew, advised that this is called a "whipstitch," the joining of two pieces of fabric together with an overcasting stitch. Excellent metaphor.

After the strained dialog between mother and daughter, Nicolette shows her maturity. From her perspective as a mother, she finds to her own surprise that she now agrees with her mother's opinion! *She* would insist on the same maturity for her daughter(s)! Nicolette next shows that she is open-minded and fair. She portrays her friend's very different conclusion about this material. Her friend —who she feels is rather like Roberta, *Walrus* character three— thought that *The Walrus* should be read in high school! Maybe her friend is right, and she is wrong. We should keep in mind that Nicolette is actually preparing the reader to ask these same questions. Her honesty induces trust.

Almost lastly, did you experience a question-bump in the *Preface*'s antepenultimate paragraph when Nicolette mentions her "kids": "twins, William and Roberta?" Why mention them at all? As writers, you don't want anything superfluous. The reader will be thinking, 'So what! Who cares what their names are?' We should ask, do these factoids add anything?

Well, mentioning the twins turns out to be apt, because just around the corner in *The Walrus*, much will revolve around the relationship between the two characters who share those names, and the claims that both they and others make about their ease of mindsharing. They *are* like twins. Nicolette is *pre-medicating* the patient. When the reader sees and hears these two characters later on, they will comfortably believe in the characters' "twinship." The reader will credit Nicolette with tying together this seeming aside in her *Preface* with later moments in *The Walrus*. It will warm them, they will smile.

From this moment on things speed up. And *keep* speeding up. A short four-line paragraph, and then the *Preface's* final paragraph. As she releases the reader from their ride on *her* rollercoaster, Nicolette launches the rocket ship dubbed, *The Walrus*. She signs off by importing five words from NASA's Mission Control: "And, ... we have lift off!"

No questions today, please. I am very tired. Exhausted.

Lecture 4: *The Walrus,* ACT I

(The Spark)

Two lectures ago I promised you a somewhat less dense exposition. Here it is. *Eccovi qua.* Here you are.

In the King James version of the *New Testament*, there is a truly memorable line which I relate to the heart of *The Walrus.* There, Saul, called Paul, later called Saint Paul, the itinerant guru of a relatively new religion, responds to a follower's inquiry by exhorting that, "Except as a thing is done with love, it is as empty as the tingling of brass."

At the play's opening we find the female lead, Jillian, kind and sweet, and occasionally feisty, and blessed with a naturally resilient and buoyant personality; but she is entirely conventional. She has never been encouraged to think independently. We learn gradually through ACT I that she had tried to make her formative relationship reciprocal and loving, but her counterpart was incapable of it. She gave without requiring that this boyfriend be worthy of the love she was willing to give and gave. She lived on hopium. Now, as a young adult, she needed —but did not consciously know it until she met the male lead— to be appreciated fully as a person within a reciprocal relationship.

This is hard to find but it does happen and because it did, Jillian increasingly realizes how undeserved the things she had done previously were. The nullity of her first's incapacity rendered her gifts "as empty as the tingling of brass."

At the play's opening we find the male lead, William, needing to be appreciated and trusted again after a not-too-distant past love affair turned disastrous. He has a bent towards humor and is confident intellectually, but he had been wounded both by the love affair that turned South as well as in childhood. He is determined not to make the mistakes of his past. This requires him, in the emotional-romantic realm, to be extremely risk-taking. He wants love and acknowledgement certainly, but he must acknowledge himself too, and *that* presents a problem in the prevailing cultural climate.

Walrus ACT I presents the step-by-step psycho-chemical reaction of hydrogen with oxygen under the gradual heat of

Jillian's and William's sexual interaction, until they combust and fuse into the water of love.

For Jillian to grow into herself, to recombine her mental DNA, the "heat" had to be applied very gradually. William intuited this and he wanted, needed, and thrilled to bring out from under the bushel basket where she hid them, Jillian's intelligence and sexuality. Yes, her sexuality! Her prior experiences bore no relation to what she experienced during the romantic events of *Walrus* ACT I with William. The male lead's demands for her to know herself, and acknowledge herself and, moreover, to confidently assert herself, were the mutative agents. Sex yes, of course, but in the long run, it was love that transformed her.

In a nutshell, that is what *Walrus* ACT I is about. It is also about patience, sacrifice and encouragement of the Other. It can and should, in my opinion, serve as a roadmap for male-female sexual encounters if love, especially young love, is the end goal. If I end my exposition of ACT I here, I would have effectively summarized the nine scenes. Nevertheless, I will give you more contrast and background.

The Walrus presents a love development in which demands for honest self-reflection and gradual attunement by the love-interest oscillate with both self-expression and self-imposed demands for patience and sacrifice. Most importantly, the play asks: To what extent is honesty possible within a committed relationship, within our culture, and how much risk can a relationship bear if the two lovers wish to truly know each other and still thrive as a couple? Risk forces new properties to emerge.

Contrast. A wide-angle shot first. Let's briefly recall *Lolita*. In *Lolita*, Nabokov grapples with the aches of a man, Humbert Humbert, who cannot grow up, cannot accept aging. "HH" is concerned exclusively with himself, even to the point of ruining a young girl, who, in some respects, he does feel tenderly about and even loves in his distorted way. "Distorted," because Humbert does *not* wish to develop her emotionally and intellectually. He does *not* prepare her for her own life.

Humbert does not thrill to the prospect of *growing* her, Lolita. He cannot free himself from his nymphet obsession. By the way, as Nabokov points out in his pseudo–prolog —his equivalent to Nicolette's *Preface*— there is not one "dirty" word in the book, yet the reader can feel Humbert's taut yearning throughout the book. But no matter how sublimely mused about in Humbert's mind, this relationship is a dead end. A tragic dead end.

The diametric opposite love development is portrayed In *The Walrus.* In it, one person tries to develop the other person, to *grow* her. He thrills to make her the *best* that she can be. He *requires* it; even at the risk of their relationship, and even foregoing certain sexual gratifications along the way. She does grow, to the point of her becoming his equal. This *despite* both the fraught honesty and the unconventional parameters of the relationship, and despite the female lead's originally unrecognized formative influences. She eventually jettisons the society-wide Stockholm Syndrome that had held her captive. She is no longer predestined to inhabit someone else's movie. She has defined herself. She has authorized herself. She challenges her helper, and their relationship thrives.

The entirety of ACT I is unrivaled in dramatizing a developing love interest. The inexorable interpenetrating of souls results in the most complete, gradual, and passionate lovemaking scenes in literature. Simply beautiful. From your point of view as aspiring writers, seize the idea that dialog and action evidence the lead's transformation. I'll illustrate this more at the end of the lecture. Equally unmatched is the second of *two* denouements in this unique play; the first occurs in ACT III and the other, its ultimate crescendo, in ACT IV. Details about those in the next two lectures.

Background. Wide-angle again. Some of you may be thinking of D. H. Lawrence's novel, *Lady Chatterley's Lover*, in which growth toward full sexual self-acceptance is made real. Body parts and actions are described, and with such love and with such attunement to the Other that it is beautiful and sounds sacred. The groundskeeper, Lady Chatterley's lover, switches registers, and addresses her with "thee" and "thou" and is especially respectful when he refers to her and his special body parts. However, the sex-love-personality development lasts for only a few pages. It is beautiful, but Linden's play offers a much more convincing *interior* development of character. And the drama is not confined to those who have the leisure for transformation, the upper-classes. Rather, Jillian is many women. She is, potentially, any girl.

Walrus ACT I is progressively elaborated over nine scenes. It is plotted developmentally with peril lurking along the way for both characters if they risk being honest. Risk they do. That is the whole point. Their souls interpenetrate organically. Couplehood and personal development go hand in hand with soul-naked risk.

I promised that this course would be a combination of both exposition and examination of writing technique. You will get the latter in abundance with next lecture, but before we leave ACT I, I want you to recall Scene 9. It is one of the most tender and exciting sex scenes-love scenes in all of literature. Jillian invites him into her apartment again, and again he declines. The dialog runs, JILLIAN: "You are stubborn." WILLIAM : "And you are the beneficiary of my discipline." Then, after a moment of hesitation, Jillian utters a remarkable four-word sentence. Note that the sentence could have been punctuated with an exclamation point, a period, or a question mark; and the difference is crucial. If an exclamation point, it would not have sounded authentically Jillian; if a period, it would have sounded flat. The question mark was *necessary* because her contending desires sound like they are *bending* into the shape of a question mark! Via the question mark, we feel Jillian's dawning confidence overcoming her inhibitions. Listen to its *music*!

William is delighted to respond affirmatively: ("Big smile. Festivities. She is happy.") For Jillian to eke out those words makes him as happy as he is to comply with her request. They then exchange an achingly taut and beautiful verbal-sexual moment that I will leave for you to re-read. The scene ends with him saying, "Goodnight," and Jillian saying, "No! Come in!" plus a bit more. William says back, "No. We're almost there. Good night."

This scene, along with Scenes 2 and 3 of ACT III, are the best love and love-making scenes in all of literature. Point- blank. I say so unapologetically! If you know of a rival, please let me know of it. Even at my ridiculous age I'd enjoy reading it.

Lecture 5: *The Walrus*, ACT II

(The Expansion)

My job is to encourage your development and to transmit knowledge. I confine myself to literary analysis. As a literary assessment therefore, and not merely as a personal opinion, I propose that *Walrus* ACTs II-IV provide the most honest and extensive discussion of sexuality within the range of couple relationships that exists in modern literature. One could even argue that it is an essay on the subject. (<u>Definition</u>: An essay; is a short analytical, descriptive or interpretive literary or journalistic prose dealing with a particular topic.) I could make the argument, but to do so would demean the drama's artistry.

Last warm-up pitch: you will recall that in *The Confession*'s Introduction, 3a, Jillian had said, speaking of *moi*,

Morton, from you and him, I got the real start of my mind. From you: What is a novel, a short story, a play, a screenplay, a prose poem, an essay? How are they different? Are the boundaries fixed or permeable?

Can a Work work, that is all of these and none alone?

Well, Jillian had done remarkable work, as had William, but it remained for Nicolette to create the assemblage that fulfilled her mother's dream. *The Bequest* contains *all* the varieties of literary endeavor in one work! It is all in one; one absolutely unique work.

Let's return, there is so much to cover.

Walrus ACT II is by far the longest act in the play. It is in this act that the wider and deeper psychological, social and moral implications are confronted. It is a dense and complicated act, necessarily so, because the issues are.

However, before detailing them, I urge you to reconsider the whole of ACT II ...musically!

As-a-unit, *Walrus* ACT II should be experienced as a fourteen-tone *arpeggio*. (Definition: arpeggio; tones of a chord produced in succession, not simultaneously.) Four long, intense scenes focus the central conflict; they are the major tones of the "chord." These are succeeded by four very short, very funny scenes. These four provide cognitive relief from the intense demands of the preceding scenes, outside of plot considerations of course. They function as "intermezzos" to refresh the cognitive palate. Next is medium length Scene 9, succeeded by three more very short scenes. Lastly, another long scene followed by a very short one. The rhythm, or pulse pattern, is lyrically interspersed. Acoustically, to my ear, *Walrus* II is like a drum solo. (Jazz aficionados —I'm one— claim to be able to tell when Max Roach is on drums.) Tune your ear to an author's rhythm signature: William's is quite different than Jillian's. This is one way we can tell them apart, both as characters and especially as authors.

ACT II, Scene 1. Ground level: the couple enjoy end–of–evening festivities again, with Jillian again being rewarded "magnificently." Remember this word from the *Preface*? Here that word is a recursive loop, *de facto* by happenstance because the playwright chose to use it and it was impossible for him to know of Nicolette's subduction of it into *The Bequest*. So Nicolette's use of "magnificently" in her *Preface* serves as foreshadow. She had to have been aware of this. As Uber-author, she was playing; intentionally setting up a long-loop, delayed-fuse "whipstitch."

Jillian says, "Come in now. Please don't be ridiculous."

Finally, William says, "I'd love to."

The gear has shifted. William wants Jillian to know him as deeply as he as knows her. He allows her the equivalent of what he has required her to unearth, regarding her sexual history and her motivations. He encourages, even implicitly demands, that she ask him anything. It is not a "kumbaya" experience. At *this* level of honesty the whole relationship is at risk!

Ask she does. The revealed truths perplex her. And these revelations portend the profound dimensions of the play.

A word appears in this act, a word that William has already *proven* to Jillian that what they have is *not* this word. Just the *opposite*! The dialog contains assertions that would have been unbelievable to Jillian had she not already had the intense yet delicate unfolding of her sexuality with William whose slow pace she had thought at the time was, "preposterous." (That word, "preposterous," occurs five times the *Preface* alone. Keep this in mind: the author was using this word too to foreshadow *The*

Walrus's dialog.) Jillian's knows, down to her core —to her innermost soul— that theirs is a love story, and not that word. Her three-to-four-month-long love affair is like nothing else she has ever known, nor even heard of, nor even dreamt about, but it is incontrovertibly *not* that word. Her new beau has even passed up what no guy would pass up. More than once. Demonstrated: a sex–love–mind story should *not* be reduced to that word. Proof has been dramatized in action. This is a deep psychological and moral love story. It is not ...a "fuckstory."

Jillian needed to have experienced a degree of sexual and emotional-spiritual intimacy that boggled her. Absent that degree of attunedness, she would have been unprepared to deal with the challenges raised by William's revelations.

Why would William reveal them? It could ruin their relationship. Jillian does not want to believe it. She can't understand it. It is so different. It is *preposterous*. It is unheard of by anyone in her reference group or dreamt of in her imagination! She must now confront a living alternative to preconceived societal expectations. William is so promoting of her growth, so caring, so normal ...how could this alternative be true? As she hears it, it sounds like nothing but a "fuckstory," and yet, it is not one. She struggles to credit it for what he says it is, but it jars her value system. It threatens her worldview!

The short of "it" is, that character three, Roberta, and William, had been lovers. And are still sometimes, occasionally. But most importantly, he contends, she is a sister–mind for him. This is extremely difficult for Jillian to wrap her mind around! Much more could be said here, but in the interest of time, I'll leave it for you to re-read the details.

Seatbelts buckled? It gets worse. Roberta has a sister, character four, Caitlin, who is living with her temporarily. The short of this "it" is, that Caitlin had confided to her sister that she only "inconsistently" orgasmed and Roberta urged Caitlin to let William guide her to her full sexual capacity! *That,* is even more difficult for Jillian to wrap her mind around! It boggles her, this time on the social and moral plane. Such unconflicted generosity? And such confidence in the outcome?! This is impossible. And it certainly must be wrong morally! One sister *pimping* for the other?

William and Roberta's two-way thing is in some way a three-way thing, with Caitlin? And the fact that William, and Roberta, are sharing all this with her, Jillian, makes it a four-way thing? Yes. But somehow, it is not perverse. Unique, or at least highly unusual, it is. But there is no suggestion of *a trois,* or of *a quatre,* nor of homosexual boundary crossing. The central dramatic conflict has been prepared: Is Jillian willing to expand her imagination to the possible reality of such honest physical and psychological soul-interpenetration?

After William's disclosures, Jillian has to interrogate. She needs him to be as open with her as she has been —*required* to be— with him. "Do you love them?" "Yes." She needs to remove any ambiguity, "Are you in love with them?" William clarifies, "No.' Within this scene is a more extensive glimpse into William's history, which I need not detail since the play focuses on Jillian and her growth and their growth as a couple.

Scene 3 ends with William asking, "Would you like to meet them?" To which Jillian says, "No! I don't know. No!"

Scene 4: The very next words we hear are Caitlin asking Roberta, "So, when are William and Jillian supposed to be here?"

All the changes that Jillian must have gone through are instantly *intuited* by the reader or audience! As I said earlier, Jillian's changes are dramatized. They are not declared by the writer. Jillian's *curiosity has won out*! She has changed her mind. The action speaks! No authorial chatter.

Next, muted light is shined on an aspect of the Roberta–William relationship. "He's probably looking for a parking spot right now. He circles the block once before parking it in a garage." Roberta's easy familiarity with him is sensed by the reader. No words declare it, no signing to the audience. She knows him that well; dramatized offhandedly. After a bare minimum of small talk, William suggests that he exit to get something for them to eat. His quick exiting is actually an affirmation of trust in Jillian although this is far from obvious at first. He respects her ability to handle herself. The couple may or may not have discussed the impending meeting —the playwright does not indicate— but William does not want to shape or influence the discussion in any way. He knows that his leaving the three women to themselves will promote a directness to the conversation. And he is right. What a conversation it is! The honesty level is breathtaking. They get to know each other at high velocity. No time is wasted.

The friends, ex-lovers or lovers, or ex-and-sometimes-lovers all aside, the thing that troubles Jillian most is that they are sisters. Roberta intuits her angst and Jillian courageously admits her distress about it. Roberta fields her concern and recontextualizes it. To Jillian's surprise, she accepts that what she hears is not nonsensical, nor preposterous, nor dirty, nor any negative value judgment that her reference group would have put on it. Dramatized: Jillian's honesty and open-mindedness, Roberta's gentleness and prowess and, obliquely, her similarity to William.

The scene expands the intimacy possibilities through the prism of two more souls. Two caring and intelligent souls. No pathology here. Jillian gets proof of this through their dialog and how they conduct themselves. Her suspicions are tentatively put to rest.

A multisided, detailed discussion ensues. Jillian asks what William has shared with them, which includes, most importantly, that he is falling in love with her. That would be with fine by itself, but Jillian wants to know if William has shared any of their intimacies with them. No and Yes. Yes, in that they, especially Roberta and William, always speak in a very open way, but, No, as both women are at pains to emphasize to Jillian, William is unfailingly respectful and uses language that suggests essence but supplies no details.

Like a cue ball breaking the rack, these encounters challenge Jillian's never-questioned value system. Most readers —who are by now strongly identified with and sympathetic to Jillian —are also implicitly challenged. The kaleidoscope lens is changed, and changed again, rapidly, as Jillian must reflect on a new, ground-shifting reality. Real people, healthy people, can live and love this way? Jillian has a lot to process. So does the reader. Society's culture-wars have been limned.

Jillian says to Roberta, both enviously and admiringly, "You know him so well," to which Roberta responds frankly, "I do." She adds, both in truth and to soothe Jillian, "You will, too. You affect him more deeply than anyone else we've seen him with. In years. He's yours. Keep letting him grow you, and in turn, you will grow him." "That's hard to believe," Jillian says, and Roberta responds, "Trust me on that, too. You will, whether you believe it now or not."

Jillian has handled herself with dignity, despite the turbulence she felt. Roberta and Caitlin have treated her and her budding relationship with William with respect. Jillian feels it. There was no rivalry here! Neither between the sisters, nor between them and her. She can feel their love for each other and their respect and love for William, and their certainty that it is reciprocated. The sexual matters were treated with delicacy, yet with no evasion. Things that everybody wants to know and what almost nobody will ask and, more pointedly, what almost nobody will talk about honestly, are discussed non-defensively. The level of intimacy and transparency is unparalleled.

There is much more fine needlework in this scene. You are groomed now; re-read it slowly, you will recognize how the writer did it. Read it slowly.

Scene 5: A Short Scene. The sisters are talking. Both have taken Jillian into their hearts. Jillian's openness, her being able to bear their honest discussion impresses them most. They know what William loves about her, and they too are charmed. At the end of a thought Roberta says to Caitlin, "And I'm getting to love her, too." And Caitlin, relishing a chance to get a small one-up on her elder sister teases, "You said before you love her. Why do you pull back, *getting to*? Why can't you just leave it that you love her?" Roberta knows, but says uncharacteristically, "I don't know," to which Caitlin rejoins, "Ughh! You're so much like him!"

Ingenuous sibling banter, a beautiful light touch functioning to give the reader another corroboration of the mind connection between Roberta and William. They *are* like twins, not just in their tastes and thinking patterns but even in their defenses. (You see how that seemingly "extraneous" detail —Nicolette's naming her twins in the *Preface*— is prodromal to the reader's heightened satisfaction at this moment?)

Scenes 6-8: Three very short, very funny scenes. Let's not destroy them by analyzing them. Savor them.

Scene 9: Medium length. Jillian is in the company of the two other women. Her musing here is reminiscent of Hamlet, soliloquizing.

Scenes 10-12: Three short scenes in which: a- Jillian has grown to the point where she can force William to recognize something; b- Caitlin gives Jillian *her* profound "gift." This gift validates both the respect Caitlin has for Jillian and her sincere wish for her and William's relationship. At the same time, it annuls society's censorious opinion of her. At the end of scene 11, Roberta too, gives Jillian a profound emotional gift. She too gives it from a place of love and respect for Jillian, and for her and William as a couple. *Nothing* more meaningful could have been given to Jillian as "a gift." Jillian appreciates the gifts, of course, if she can trust them, but she does not yet recognize the full impact that both women are having on her psyche. That will manifest in Acts III and IV. And c- William recontextualizes the soul-meaning of Caitlin's original promise to him, transforming its surface value. Jillian believes him, although it requires all of her objectivity and trust to do so. The lead characters are growing both separately and as a couple.

Scenes 13-14: Jillian is coming to understand the meaning, and beauty, of the inner experiences they are all now sharing. And she is coming to understand William's essential nature.

We must stop here. I must rest. I'm tired all the time lately.

...Oh the bell hasn't rung yet. Ten minutes. Screw being tired! So I'll die tomorrow. Or the next day.

Next lecture covers ACTs III through V. As prelude to it, I must alert you to a heartrending scene: ACT III Scene 4. Jillian apologizes for her argument in ACT III Scene 1, and then William discloses some moments from his history. He gives her just a few vignettes, but his emergence from that background corroborates Roberta's earlier assurance to Jillian, (ACT II Scene 11), that William worked hard to overcome his defenses that were a consequence of the impact of ceaseless indoctrination and drubbings that he had been subjected to. The playwright provides only these tiny glimpses of what had happened throughout his childhood, but they are a disheartening and even frightening chord that introduces Jillian to his past. We hear its authenticity. Lucky for him that he had a brother, and they could support each other. We, the reader, embellish by induction. The glimpses induce our conviction of truth.

Meta-level and from a literary point of view, had he gone further into his history that would have de-centered our attention from Jillian. It is good thing too that Nicolette, as Uber-author, chose not to elaborate on what she must have known from her mother about her father's history. His revelations were sufficient.

Thank you, Nicolette, for not adding anything. It is better. In this case, less is truly, more.

Oh, I see that we still have a few minutes. Your door prize for attending today is something that I bet all of you missed. You really must become close readers. Literature of this quality demands that you turn every facet of text to the light —like jewelers examining the interior of the Star of India diamond— in order to experience the full sparkle of the material. We know from *The Preface* dialog that Nicolette's father had selected six citations: Jillian had let Nicolette read only that one-page morsel, We know this from text, because Nicolette commented on them. William must have wanted the citations to introduce *The Walrus.* But that doesn't work with drama. The play must speak for itself. So, we must conclude that Nicolette found them suitable for her own work and that once again she repurposed them by making them part of the warm-up notes for *The Bequest* as-a-whole. The last citation was an honorarium to her parents. Thus, the citations became her seven-tone "arpeggio."

Lecture 6: *The Walrus*, ACTs III – V

(The Regression, The Second Expansion, The Engagement)

In ACTs III and IV we witness Jillian's further evolution. She speaks more confidently and behaves more independently. Her growth can only be accounted for by the self-confrontational work she had to have done to reach this level. Dialog and action, as always, dramatize the change. I will speed through some of the action here since you understand *The Walrus*'s framework. We have only so much time. There is simply too much intricacy to unpack leisurely.

Scene 1: Jillian's apartment. Jillian has been struggling to process all that happened with Roberta and Caitlin as well as with William's further explanation of both how he loves and his relationship with those women. Jillian is obviously in love and desperately trying to make sense of it all but is still in the grip of her received value system. She regresses and provokes an argument. The scene represents the last grasp of her confining chrysalis before she breaks free to emerge as a butterfly, an adult.

Even though he is afraid of where this could go, and even when she briefly waxes irrational, William reacts to her respectfully. Jillian calms down due to his balanced handling of her and the conversation evolves into an emerging recognition on Jillian's part that the expectations she had from her earlier life —expectations both conscious and previously unconscious— have been inadequate. The interpenetration level deepens as both characters reveal and demand with soul-naked honesty.

Had William reacted differently Jillian would not have calmed down and they might even have broken up. Jillian appreciates his ability to weather her storm and then uses his groundedness to restabilize herself. This reciprocity models how their relationship will thrive —eventually as a two-way street— which will shortly be demonstrated and acknowledged.

There is so much more in this scene but not enough time to unpack it further. You have a head start now. Re-read it.

Scenes 2 and 3 are, I remind you, the most beautiful, tender and erotic in all of literature. They are a model for female-male sexuality based on trust and soul-interpenetration. Savor them.

Scene 4: Jillian's apology and the segue into William's further revelation of his background and development. This is the scene of which I forewarned you. This scene was necessary because, on ground level, Jillian needed some history to sink her teeth into. She had to know more about William and his struggle to arise from a troubled childhood.

On the meta level, the playwright *had* to include this scene so that the reader would find William plausible and to have evidence of his work on himself. Note that William's words to Jillian here, match almost exactly Roberta's words to her in ACT II, Scene 11. Cross-validation.

Scene 5: Jillian is growing. She comes right out and says to Caitlin, "I'm practicing talking like you ... so I'll jump right to the point." Caitlin replies, "I'm flattered. " But quickly adds, "I think," to lighten the mood. Jillian explains that she wants to experience

Caitlin without Roberta around. Caitlin advises, "I *am* a separate person, you know." This definite but gentle pushback reinforces the idea that she has her own identity and is not living in her sister's shadow.

A bit more interaction and then down to brass tacks. Jillian needs Caitlin to reveal more about her experience of William. To talk about *that* they need a different venue! She suggests they walk over to Central Park.

Future writers, be aware that Nicolette is doing two things at once here! On ground level, as Jillian and Caitlin are deciding which bench to sit on, two tiny, but very significant side lights are lit up. The first playfully reinforces the essential brother-sister minds of William and Roberta, and the second spotlights Nicole Krauss' novel, *The History of Love*, which all four have read and both William and Roberta love.

Meta level: The mention of Nicole Krauss' novel within the context of Jillian's and Caitlin's interaction here in *Walrus* Act III, brief as it is, will give enhanced authenticity to the hilarious and passionate discussion of that book later, in Part 3b of Jillian's *My Confession*; that is, her dialog with Morton. In this way, it is a foreshadow. Remember; Jillian at this moment in her life hasn't the faintest idea that she will write *anything* literary, let alone the dramatic masterpiece, 3b, contained within *The Confession.* She wrote that years later! She has to raise a child who she does not yet know she is pregnant with, Nicolette.

I know that I gave you earlier an overview of how Nicolette "anchored and buttressed" her work as a whole. But this novel requires a higher resolution analysis. When you go back to re-read *The Bequest* you will recognize that Nicolette has been lashing the sides of her Tower together with narrative silk since the beginning, and you hadn't realized it. No one does, on first reading! Not even *moi.* Her two-steps forward and one-step back approach in the *Preface* directly connects to *The Walrus*, Part 2. There, the reader immediately loses sight of Nicolette and her *Preface*, which she wanted. The conversations that occurred within the *Preface* bind with Jillian's *Confession*, Part 3, and with Jillian's *Journal*, Part 4. This, *PSLS,* Part 5, is winched together with her *Preface* by means of the *Morton and Jillian Discuss the Title* dialog, as well as with her mentioning of Morton in the *Prolog* to the Preface.

Scene 6: Jillian is alone with Roberta here. As if the preceding scene were not incredible enough, this scene tops it! The deepest aspects of their core selves are discussed with yet *more* breathtaking honesty. Jillian summons her courage and risks asking Roberta *the* most personal and significant question she can ask of any woman, especially this one. Jillian pushes the question out. Roberta responds by telling her that she will tell her two stories. "About him? About him and you?" Jillian asks naturally, and wrongly. "No," Roberta tells her, "about this topic, and it should help you clear up whatever you're working on."

Both stories are point blank intimate revelations! Roberta's truthfulness commands Jillian's respect and her clarity and decisiveness are even more impactful. They overcome any doubts that might have lingered in Jillian's mind about Roberta's integrity. Roberta's actions are a model for Jillian. Jillian is fully satisfied, grateful, even astonished at Roberta's honesty and willingness to share at this level. As the scene ends they exchange gentle smiles. They too have become sisters and this bond will affect both her and William and reciprocally, all four of them. Demonstrated once again: the "Willing Interpenetration of Souls."

ACT IV, Scene 1: This scene and the next are the only normally paced ones in the play. By comparison, they seem slow-moving. All the participants in the future engagement party are present, and the talk is about Jillian's wedding plans and dress choices.

Scene 2: A brief scene, some more banter between William and Jillian, with Jillian showing more strength. She softly challenges William. Light tones continue before the next electrifying scene.

Scene 3: Jillian and William are away on a vacation. They have had their usual extensive and magical love play. William offers her some pot. Jillian agrees to try it in the safety of their relationship.

Before I continue, I remind you that this unique play has *two* denouements. The first occurred in ACT III, Scene 1, where Jillian uses the word, "transactionally," as her own, in a new and fully understood context. She had processed it from the middle of ACT II, Scene 11, where she hadn't fully understood Roberta's use of it. In this transition moment, she even teases William with her confident use of it. All the internal psychological work Jillian must have done is dramatized. Jillian has grown.

And the second denouement occurs in ACT IV Scene 3 and is the following: Jillian and William are away, playing and relaxing. William purposely makes another obvious verbal "mistake." Jillian rolls right with him this time, using his "mistake" to equal him and neutralize him. Playful, nice, tender. The next morning, they are luxuriating in their playspace when Jillian gets a shock: She remembers a dream. She will never forget it. It is eidetic!

She describes it to William. She asks for his help to understand it, if possible. Rather than leaping to interpret it, he walks her through some steps so that she might interpret it herself. After several piecemeal steps, she starts to feel something. "What?" he asks. "*Intense* joy and *intense* shame. It's the *weirdest* combination! It's so *intense*!" Jillian gasps. William asks, "Can you get the rest by yourself?" No. He leads her, until Jillian, recognizing the meaning of the dream, has an all-encompassing catharsis.

When she subsides but *before* she speaks, William says, "Thank you." To *her*. What has happened is beyond what he has been hoping for and working for. It is even more complete than he had imagined. The reader shares the joy that he feels for her. No further dialog or description is needed than, "Thank you. Thank you so much." The reader *knows* everything they need to know.

On the heels of this moment, yet *another* moment of supreme induction follows on! Her voice barely above a whisper, Jillian says, "*Me*?" "Thank *you*. I thank *you*." (pause, whisper) "For taking away my ...you know." William jumps in, "I know." (Silence) The reader knows too. *All* has been induced in the reader's mind. Any half-awake soul would know! He did not need her to specify. Her transformation is complete. He spares her. Jillian has recognized what he wished her to recognize. The soul-contact between the characters is instantaneous. "Thank you. I thank *you*."

Scene 4: A few weeks later, in her apartment, Jillian begins a conversation that no one would have any idea of where it will go —certainly not William! Her discussion reflects enormous growth. She makes an extraordinary proposal! *He* is astonished, delighted, and flabbergasted; and, profoundly grateful. He knows that Jillian, previously, would have thought anyone dreaming *this* up was being "preposterous." But Jillian now knows herself and William well enough —soul deep— that she can live in *her* own newly defined worldspace. She is her own person. Others matter; but she matters too now; and in intimate matters, she matters more.

Scene 5: More demonstration of Jillian's growth. She is fully William's equal here. She initiates a challenge: for him to place their relationship and the four-way *pas de quatre* in a long-term time frame. She tells him, "Hon, you've got a lot of soul-searching to do." He acknowledges and tries to lighten the moment by using comedy again, jive talk, "Jillian, you are good. So good, you *baaad*." She is unashamedly confident, "Yep. I *baaad*."

ACT V, Scene 1: The joyous engagement party on a meadow in Central Park.

Scene 2: The tragedy. William's death by gunshot by his Ex-.

Obviously, under the circumstances, Jillian had to be the author of ACT V. She recounted what she could of the story, (just as Hamlet had bid Horatio to do).

Just as an interesting tidbit —and this I'm sure was *un*planned— Hamlet also dies in ACT V Scene 2.

This is a perfect place to stop. Whew. I'm out of steam anyway. Next week, an analysis of Jillian's *Confession.*

Lecture 7: Jillian's *Confession*

For those of you who don't know me, I am Nicolette Linden, Dr. Seiden's assistant. Morton has died. A memorial service will be held this Saturday at the Unitarian Church in Brooklyn Heights. For today I will lead the class in an abbreviated session. Starting next week Mei Jing Lu, visiting professor on sabbatical from Beijing University, has generously agreed to finish the semester for him.

---- A minute of silence, please. Let us savor all that he gave us.----

Little more could be added to Morton's analysis. I can give you only bits and pieces, but you may find them worth thinking about.

In Lecture 2, Morton opined that there were at least seven levels by his count to the construction of *The Bequest*. Why did he say that: "by my count?" Could someone else have counted differently? For your convenience, I've printed out that part of his lecture:

"There are seven levels of Imagination and Intention operating right now. Right now, I am teaching you:

1) how to recognize techniques that some talented writers have used to make their texts vivid and coherent;

2) how to read and deconstruct text generally;

3) how Nicolette's all-important framing narrative allowed her to introduce both her father's play *The Walrus* and

4) her mother's work *The Confession,* as well as Jillian's *Journal;*

5) how Nicolette subtly mirrors her mother's metatextual device by incorporating me into the story. ...To remind you, in Jillian's play I was an unwitting accomplice; in this, Nicolette's novel, I knew what she was doing and, frankly, marveled at it.

6) how Nicolette utilized these lectures to provide a literary anatomy lesson on the dissection of a multilayered novel and thereby, how to deconstruct and even reverse engineer a complex work of literature, and, most importantly;

7) how all three writers set for themselves a very, *very* high bar of Imagination to vault. There may be another intention, an eighth level, to Nicolette's recursive metafiction but that is a speculation for a later lecture.

You know Morton's style by now. He avoided speaking with throwaway lines. You know that he did not insert extra flourishes to be cute. So we should at least entertain the notion that he put in that phrase, "by my count," to come back to it at some later point, and when he did, he would use it as a long-delayed "whipstitch" to pull things together for the student. The return would serve as a heuristic device planted to induce the student to think, "What were those levels, exactly?" And the student who cares would then have to recall the story and, thereby, remember Morton's analysis of it.

Since Morton was not given to making mere nice touches, I know that he believed there was at least one more level and that it has to do with the writer's, or writers', motivation. I know this from my precious time with him, listening to him, and preparing these lectures. Factually, there were three writers of *The Bequest*: me, my mother, and my father. I have explained my motivation in the *Preface* and Morton has so brilliantly explicated some techniques I used to weave the parts into an organic whole. Mom stipulated her motivation in the *Reprise*. So, that leaves only William, my father.

There is one particular line in Jillian's *Confession* that I am certain *no one* pays attention to. It is mysteriously potent though; the line where she addresses Nicole Krauss directly: "If my work is seven-tenths of yours, I am happy." Undoubtedly, a reader chalks this up to an admirer's excessive praise. But I don't think so. Why that number? Mom, like Morton, didn't indulge in throwaways. Just the opposite. For documentation, recall or reread how she spoke during our "Snag."

Morton made one passing reference to a speculation of Mom's. Jillian had wondered if besides everything *else* it was doing, *The Walrus* might have been a protest to his Ex-. Mom never discussed this with me. I could be wrong, but personally, I don't think so. The intensity of his play is focused on Mom and him, her growth, and their growth as a couple. But if it is so, that would be an eighth level, merely an additional motivation that did no harm to the corpus of the overall play. Nevertheless, Morton would not have revealed this to me if he didn't want me to think about it and I bring it up to you as future writers for the same reason.

One last thing. Jillian was my Mom, so obviously I knew her very well. But I have an X- ray of *both* my parents' minds and their relationship via their plays. Also, I have, if I may use this term, a preternatural sense of my father's personality. I am rather like him, mentally, Mom told me. To jump to the point, I have a feeling about there being at least one further level to *The Walrus* —a hologram that becomes visible only with a laser beam of intuition.

I will leave you with this.... In, *Fermat's Last Theorem,* Simon Singh describes the grueling work of ten years that the mathematician, Andrew Weil, needed to prove Fermat's theorem. Fermat had left a notation in the margin of his journal, "I have proof of this, but I don't have space to write it here." Utterly baffling in the extreme. For three hundred years, the world's brightest minds could not solve the problem. Also agonizingly tantalizing is the story in the middle of Singh's book —probably the invention of a talented wag— where a student waiting for a subway train in New York had written on the wall, "I have proof of Fermat's last theorem ...but my train is coming."

It took three hundred years to solve Fermat's last theorem. And the solution invented a new area of mathematics.

Is there another level ?

That I have already hinted to you. ...Yes.

Is there another level yet ...beyond that? Or two?

Oh, look ...here comes my train.